NAMIBIA
THE FACTS

IDAF PUBLICATIONS LTD.
A publishing company of
International Defence and Aid Fund for Southern Africa
London, 1989

All photographs are from the photo library of IDAF Publications and Audio-Visual Department.

The International Defence and Aid Fund for Southern Africa is a humanitarian organisation which has worked consistently for peaceful and constructive solutions to the problems created by racial oppression in Southern Africa.

It sprang from Christian and humanist opposition to the evils and injustices of apartheid in Southern Africa. It is dedicated to the achievement of free, democratic, non-racial societies throughout Southern Africa.

The objects of the Fund are:-

(i)   to aid, defend and rehabilitate the victims of unjust legislation and oppressive and arbitrary procedures,

(ii)   to support their families and dependents,

(iii)   to keep the conscience of the world alive to the issues at stake.

In accordance with these three objects, the Fund distributes its humanitarian aid to the victims of racial injustice without any discrimination on grounds of race, colour, religious or political affiliation. The only criterion is that of genuine need.

The Fund runs a comprehensive information service on affairs in Southern Africa; this includes visual documentation. The Fund prides itself on the strict accuracy of all its information. Associated with IDAF is a publishing company IDAF Publications Ltd. which produces a regular news bulletin FOCUS on Political Repression in Southern Africa. It also publishes pamphlets and books and produces films and photographic exhibitions on all aspects of repression and resistance in Southern Africa.

This book was prepared by IDAF Research, Information and Publications Department.

ISBN No. 0 904759 946
British Library C.I.P. Data I. IDAF 968.8'03

Printed in England by A. G. Bishop & Sons Ltd., Orpington, Kent.

CONTENTS

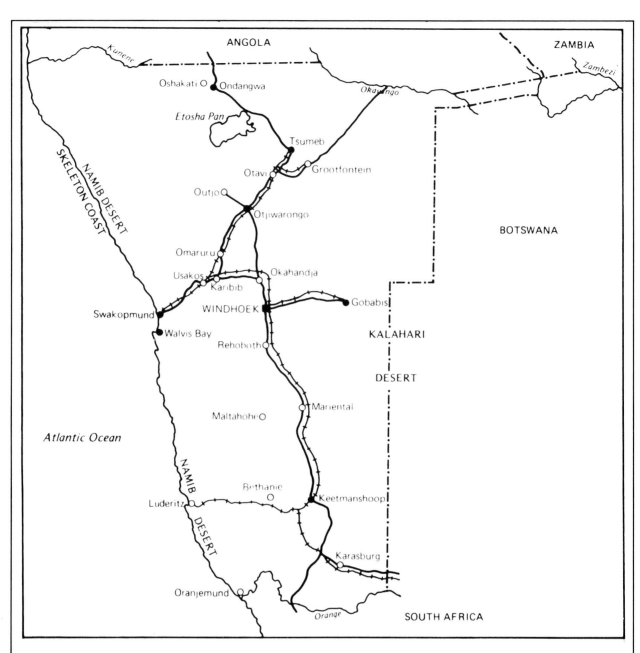

ANGOLA

ZAMBIA

Kunene

Oshakati ○ ●Ondangwa

Okavango

Zambezi

Etosha Pan

Tsumeb

Otavi ○Grootfontein

Outjo ○

Otjiwarongo

BOTSWANA

SKELETON COAST

NAMIB DESERT

Omaruru ○

Usakos ○ Okahandja

Karibib ○

Swakopmund

WINDHOEK ■ ●Gobabis

●Walvis Bay

Rehoboth ○

KALAHARI

DESERT

Atlantic Ocean

Maltahohe ○

Mariental ○

NAMIB

Bethanie ○

DESERT

Luderitz

Keetmanshoop

Karasburg ○

Oranjemund ○

Orange

SOUTH AFRICA

NAMIBIA

- ■● MAJOR TOWNS
- ○ OTHER TOWNS
- —— MAJOR ROADS
- +++++ RAILWAYS
- ⌒⌒ PERENNIAL RIVERS

0   200

KILOMETRES

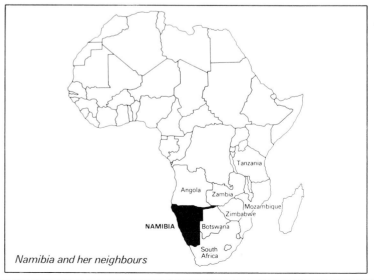

Tanzania

Angola Zambia

Mozambique

Zimbabwe

NAMIBIA Botswana

South
Africa

Namibia and her neighbours

PREFACE

This book presents the facts about Namibia, a vast semi-arid territory under South African occupation. It replaces an earlier IDAF publication of the same title and forms a companion volume to *Apartheid: The Facts*, which examines apartheid in South Africa.

Namibia is occupied illegally by South Africa, which has imposed its apartheid system of racist segregation and minority rule. The United Nations is responsible for ensuring Namibian independence, but South Africa has refused to end its occupation. It maintains its rule by force. Tens of thousands of troops enforce repressive laws and terrorise Namibia's one and a half million people.

Namibia was colonised by Germany more than a hundred years ago. South Africa invaded the country during the First World War and made it effectively a colony. Today Namibia is the last country in Africa still under colonial control.

South Africa's occupation of Namibia was declared illegal by the UN in 1966 and by the International Court of Justice five years later. After negotiations with the South African government the UN Security Council, by Resolution 435, set out an agreed plan for independence. However, South Africa has refused to implement this plan. Namibian independence is thus one of the major concerns of the UN and the international community.

The Namibian people have always resisted colonial rule. The national liberation movement, the South West Africa People's Organisation (SWAPO) was formed in 1960 and is recognised by the UN as the sole and authentic representative of the Namibian people on whose behalf it took up arms in 1966 to fight for freedom.

SWAPO has been harshly repressed inside Namibia, but it has continued to mobilise people into the freedom struggle. In churches, trade unions, and youth, student and women's organisations, the Namibian people are united behind SWAPO's demand for independence.

Namibians are at war with the South African occupation forces. Guerrillas operate throughout the country, but especially in the northern areas, where more than half the population live.

The South African occupation has devastated Namibia. More than ten thousand people have been killed. Over one hundred thousand have been forced into exile or become refugees in neighbouring countries. The vast majority of Namibians face poverty and unemployment, and are discriminated against in all areas of life. With few exceptions the tiny minority of people classified as white, many of them South African settlers, have benefited, along with South African and transnational companies which exploit Namibia's natural and human resources.

Namibian independence is one of the most pressing responsibilities of the international community, the struggle of a nation to be free and to determine its own future. It is a vital component of the struggle against racism and apartheid.

TERMINOLOGY & STATISTICS

Accurate statistics about many aspects of Namibia are difficult to obtain. The South African authorities neglect to monitor key social and economic indices, and where statistics are produced they are often distorted to disguise the negative effects of the South African occupation.

UN agencies and other bodies, with assistance from SWAPO and independent researchers, have calculated figures on the basis of models, projections and estimates drawn from the limited concrete data available. These estimates are used in this book where statistics provided by the South African authorities are not reliable.

Apartheid has led to a variety of terms to describe the divisions it has imposed on the population. Many of these are used by the regime in South Africa, while others have been specifically devised for Namibia.

Wherever possible, the language of apartheid has been avoided, although it is not possible to describe the situation in Namibia without at times making some use of apartheid concepts and terms.

All Namibians who have been historically disenfranchised and oppressed are termed 'black' in this book. People classified 'white' in apartheid terms are referred to as such.

The term 'African' is used in the early chapters to describe Namibia's pre-colonial inhabitants. In this period the various African societies are referred to by their historically accepted names such as 'Herero' and 'Nama', which should be distinguished from the present-day apartheid usage of these terms.

The black population has been divided into 11 separate 'population groups' by the apartheid regime but no such distinction is made in this book unless it is unavoidable.

Each 'group' in Namibia has a separate administration, referred to as second-tier administrations, and according to their official titles e.g. Administration for Whites, Administration for Ovambos.

Most of the second-tier administrations are based in geographic areas which are called 'homelands' by the South African authorities, and which are referred to in this book as 'bantustans', as is common in Namibia. These areas were allocated to each of the black 'groups' in order to leave the whites in clear control of the central administration and the bulk of the land.

1 HISTORICAL BACKGROUND

The political domination and exploitation of the black population of Namibia have evolved from the colonial conquest of the territory. Repression and discrimination have existed since the first years of colonialism in the area.

PRE-COLONIAL HISTORY

The pre-colonial inhabitants of central Namibia herded vast numbers of cattle. Further south where the vegetation is drier, sheep and goats were kept, while in the flood plains of the north and in better-watered parts of the north-east, people settled densely on the land and grew millet and other crops. In the driest parts of the country communities survived by hunting game and gathering food. Copper, salt and iron were mined in various places.

The different African communities were bound by political alliances and trade, although there were periodic conflicts over grazing and other rights.

COLONIAL CONQUEST

The rough seas and harsh desert along Namibia's coastline kept out European traders and colonists, who made only limited incursions into the territory during the sixteenth and seventeenth centuries. However, the aggressive expansion of British settlement from the Cape began to disrupt southern and central Namibia during the eighteenth century as people were displaced northwards.

Christian missionaries and traders began to penetrate Namibia from the Cape. New economic and military forces destroyed the stability of Namibian societies and led to political and social divisions.

In the second half of the

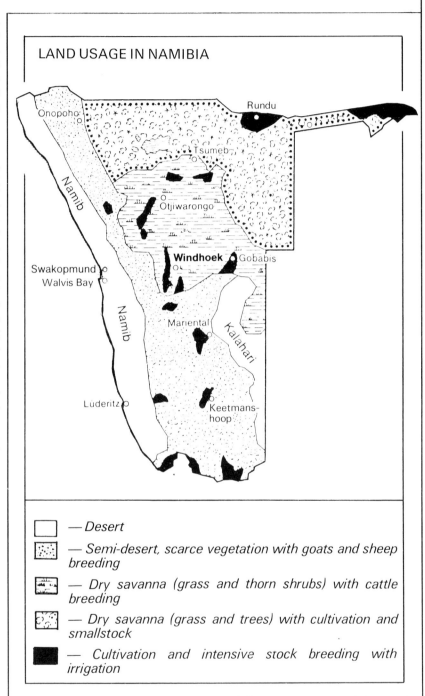

LAND USAGE IN NAMIBIA

— Desert

— Semi-desert, scarce vegetation with goats and sheep breeding

— Dry savanna (grass and thorn shrubs) with cattle breeding

— Dry savanna (grass and trees) with cultivation and smallstock

— Cultivation and intensive stock breeding with irrigation

Namibia has always been sparsely populated. Half of the land is desert or semi-desert, and it has the driest climate in Africa south of the Sahara. The country is divided into three main geographic regions. The harsh Namib desert stretches along the Atlantic coast to a distance of 80 to 130 kilometres inland. The sands and rocky outcrops of the Namib give way to an inland plateau, broken in places by barren mountain ranges. The plateau slopes eastwards to the basin of the Kalahari Desert, the fringes of which form the third major environmental region in Namibia. Apart from isolated pockets, only in the north is there sufficient water for growing crops.

nineteenth century Britain annexed the natural harbour of Walvis Bay and a German company gained control of Luderitz Bay. The colonial status of Namibia, like that of many African countries, was decided by the European powers at the Conference of Berlin in 1884-5 where, with the exception of Walvis Bay, the territory was allocated to Germany. The boundaries of German South West Africa, as Namibia was then known, were formalised over the following few years, cutting across existing patterns of settlement.

Berlin Conference

Armed German colonists moved into the southern and central areas, depriving the inhabitants of land on which to graze their cattle. Resistance was hindered by disunity, although in 1858 African leaders came together at Hoachanas, and signed a treaty which set out procedures for resolving differences. But the Germans fomented divisions by making and breaking military and economic agreements with the various communities to further their control, and only temporary and limited unity was achieved against German domination.

By 1903, more than half the herds previously owned by the Herero people, who lived in the central areas of Namibia, had passed into the hands of settlers. Many Africans, whose traditional livelihood had been undermined, were forced to take up waged labour for the colonists, usually on a temporary or migrant basis.

Peace Treaty of Hoachanas, 1858 (extracts)

In the name of the Holy Trinity, the Father and the Son and the Holy Ghost, we the undersigned have resolved to unite in the following treaty:

No chief with his people will have the right, should a dispute arise between him and another chief of standing, to pursue his own vindication, but shall be pledged to bring the case before an impartial court.

When the case has been examined by the impartial chiefs, the guilty party shall be punished or a fine shall be imposed upon him. Should he be unwilling to comply with the judgement and should he attempt to dispute the issue by force of arms, then shall all the treaty chiefs be pledged jointly to take up arms and punish him . . .

No chief may permit copper being mined in his territory without the knowledge and agreement of all other chiefs, or to sell a farm or site within his territory to a white person from the Cape Colony. Whoever despite this makes such a sale shall be heavily fined, and the purchaser himself will have to bear the cost if he has been acquainted with this law beforehand.

Signed by seventeen Namibian leaders from the south and central parts of the country

GENOCIDE

In January 1904, provoked by the continuing seizure of their lands, the Herero rose against the Germans. Lacking firearms and unable to move quickly because of their large herds of cattle, they were defeated and driven eastwards into the waterless Kalahari desert. In August, the Nama, who lived mainly in the south of the country, joined the war under the leadership of Hendrik Witbooi. By adopting guerrilla tactics, a Nama commando under Jacob Morenga was able to continue fighting until 1906.

The German colonial authorities, determined to wipe out resistance, resorted to genocide, poisoning water-holes and machine-gunning refugees. Through such methods they reduced the population of central and southern Namibia by more than half. Survivors were forced into prison labour camps on the coast, where thousands more died. The societies in central and southern Namibia were devastated. Legislation was introduced depriving Africans of the right to own land or cattle. Leaders who were not killed were exiled or silenced.[1]

German colonial troops in Windhoek

General Von Trotha (right)

I, the great general of the German troops, send this letter to the Herero people.

Hereros are no longer German subjects . . . All the Hereros must leave the land. If the people do not want this, then I will force them to do it with the great guns. Any Herero found within the German borders with or without a gun, with or without cattle, will be shot. I shall no longer receive any women or children; I will drive them back to their people or I will shoot them. This is my decision for the Herero people.

— The Great General of the Mighty Kaiser

Proclamation of 2 October 1904 issued by General Von Trotha

Survivors of the German genocide

Through the quiet night we heard, in the distance, the lowing of enormous herds of thirsty cattle, and a dull, confused sound like the movement of a whole people. To the east there was a gigantic glow of fire. The enemy had fled to the east with their whole enormous mass – women, children, and herds.

The next morning we ventured to pursue the enemy. The ground was trodden down into a floor for a width of about a 100 yards, for in such a broad thick horde had the enemy and their herds of cattle stormed along. In the path of their flight lay blankets, skins, ostrich feathers, household utensils, women's ornaments, cattle, and men – dead and dying and staring blankly . . .

A number of babies lay helplessly languishing by mothers whose breasts hung down long and flabby. Others were lying alone, still living, with eyes and nose full of flies. Somebody sent out our black drivers and I think they helped them to die. All this life lay scattered there, both men and beasts, broken in the knees, helpless, still in agony, or already motionless . . .

At noon we halted by water-holes which were filled to the brim with corpses.

Description by a German soldier of the pursuit of the Herero (quoted in Melber, 1983, p. 76)

All our obedience and patience with the Germans avails us nothing. My brother, do not go back on your word and stay out of the fighting, but rather let all the people fight against the Germans and let us be resolved to die together rather than to be killed by the Germans through mistreatment, imprisonment, or some other way. Further, you should inform all your captains who are subject to you that they too should stand and fight.

Letter from Samuel Maharero to Hendrik Witbooi

The Nama warriors showed unbelievable stamina and mobility, decided skill in the use of terrain in guerrilla warfare, and last but not least great personal courage.

Extract from records of the German General Staff

Hendrik Witbooi

Samuel Maharero

Witbooi and his troops

Jacob Morenga

— Do you think this war will continue long?
— Yes, certainly, as long as there is a man on the field.
— Do you know that Germany is one of the mightiest military powers in the world?
— Yes, I am aware of it; but they cannot fight in our country. They do not know where to get water, and do not understand guerrilla warfare.

Newspaper interview with Jacob Morenga, May 1906

It took the full resources of German colonialism in Namibia to subjugate the Herero and Nama, and the densely populated north was never conquered but left largely under the control of independent African kingdoms. Through economic pressures, the Germans were able to obtain migrant labour from these areas.

COLONIAL EXPLOITATION

Until the turn of the century German interest in Namibia centred on expropriating African land and establishing military and political control over the southern and central parts of the territory, which were set aside for colonial settlement. This area was called the Police Zone as it was controlled largely through a network of police and military posts.

Despite the seizure of land, most Africans were still able to survive through traditional farming and herding activities. The colonists found it difficult to recruit labour for settler farms and for building the harbours, roads and railways they needed. They increasingly resorted to the forced labour of prisoners captured in military expeditions against the local people, and to short-term contract workers recruited from the north, where trading debts were obliging the local rulers to act as labour recruiters.

Forced Labour

The genocide of 1904-7 left the countryside in ruins, and the German governor, Leutwein, himself remarked that his troops had 'destroyed' two-thirds of the potential labour force. In 1906 commercial copper mining began at Tsumeb, but it was the discovery of diamonds in the southern Namib desert two years later which led to a sudden interest in the exploitation of the colony's resources. Exports from Namibia rose from a mere 400,000 Marks in 1906 to nearly 35 million Marks in 1910.[2]

Africans in the Police Zone were forced to work for the colonists through the 1907 Labour Code. This denied them the right to own land or livestock and compelled them to work at whatever tasks they were allotted by the colonial administration.

By 1910 it was estimated that 85 per cent of African males in the Police Zone were working for whites. However, thousands of Africans escaped into neighbouring Botswana, and many managed to regroup secretly in remote areas and resume livestock farming.[3]

After largely unsuccessful efforts to recruit labour from neighbouring colonies, the German authorities concentrated on increasing the supply of labour from the north. Between 1907 and 1910, the migrant labour force increased fourfold to 6,000.[4]

Migrant workers were kept under close control and isolated in barrack-like compounds. Wages were kept low – in 1913 the wage bill of the diamond companies amounted to a mere 2 per cent of the value of diamonds mined.

Workers on settler farms were kept in conditions of virtual slavery. They were unpaid, and a survey conducted in 1912 revealed that on most farms the food issued to workers was inadequate to sustain them and their families.[5] Settlers were legally empowered to administer corporal punishment to workers, who were often flogged to the

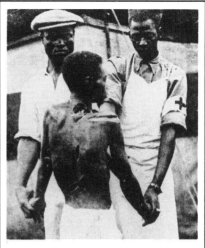

point of death.[6]

In 1913 the authorities began to set up 'reserves' on government-owned farms in order to restrict Namibians to small areas, to exert political and economic control and to ensure a supply of labour. The system also fragmented political leadership.[7]

By the time the First World War broke out, the basic structure of what would become the apartheid system in Namibia was already well established. Africans from the north were employed on a migrant- or contract-labour basis and kept rigidly segregated, while in the Police Zone Africans had either been forced to work on white-owned farms or were being settled into impoverished 'reserves'. Africans had very few political or social rights in the land of their birth. Almost all the stock-farming land was in the hands of white settlers while profits from the mines flowed to shareholders and owners overseas.

The basic features of this colonial system were to change little in the following decades.

SOUTH AFRICA INVADES

In 1915 South Africa invaded German South West Africa on behalf of the British Empire, of which it was then a part. Thirteen thousand South African troops easily subdued the smaller German garrison, and the territory was placed under a South African military governor.

At the Treaty of Versailles, the colonies of defeated Imperial Germany were placed under the authority of Britain, France or their allies, under a mandate system administered by the League of Nations. 'Full powers of administration and legislation' over Namibia were conferred on the British crown, 'for and on behalf of' the Union of South Africa.[8]

The government in Pretoria was charged with administering the territory as a 'sacred trust of civilisation' and for the 'well-being and development' of the indigenous population. It was prohibited from establishing military bases in Namibia or conscripting the population for military service. Its administration would be supervised by the Permanent Mandates Commission established by the League of Nations.

German officials, soldiers and police in Namibia were deported to Germany, but at least half the German population was allowed to remain. The South African government wanted simply to annex the new territory and rule it as part of the Union, but as a result of international and domestic pressures this was not possible.

The South African Prime Minister, General Smuts, consoled those clamouring for incorporation with the argument that 'the relations between the South West Protectorate and the Union amount to annexation in all but name'.[9]

THE NEW COLONIALISTS

As German rule collapsed, the black population in the Police Zone recovered some livestock and demanded the return of their lands. But Pretoria regarded its new territory as a colony, ripe for the settlement of white farmers. Loans and other incentives were made available and immigration from South Africa was promoted. Settlers streamed into the territory, including a group of Afrikaners who had previously settled in Portuguese Angola. The new colonists were allocated huge farms on the rich grazing lands of the central plateau.

By 1926 the white population had almost doubled from the war years, despite the repatriation of many Germans. Nearly a thousand farms had been established, covering a large part of the country – the average white farm was 37,000 acres (15,000 hectares).[10]

The new administration, following the model being established in South Africa, intensified efforts to force Africans into small and infertile reserves. The Herero were allocated stretches of semi-desert in the east – the same area in which thousands had died during the retreat from the Germans in 1904.

Hardly any economic development took place in the reserves. More money was spent on settling just one group of white farmers – Afrikaners who were brought from Angola – than was spent on the entire African population in the ten years between 1928 and 1938.[11]

In the period 1925-32, twelve times as much was spent on the education of the white population as on the black population; in 1934 the annual per capita expenditure on education was 25 times higher for white children than for black children.[12] Even in the mines, where funds were abundant, poor medical, health, housing and dietary conditions persisted. Pneumonia and scurvy were common.[13]

Segregation was also enforced in urban areas, where Africans were made to live on the outskirts of towns in 'locations', which after 1928 were controlled by local white municipalities.[14]

The South African administration denigrated German colonialism as barbaric but continued many of the old policies. Laws applicable to Africans – usually laws in force in South Africa which were extended to Namibia by proclamation – had the same effect as the German laws.

Africans were forbidden to own land; livestock ownership was limited by law and restricted by grazing fees. Hunting was also restricted by taxes on the dogs which were used to chase game. Curfews were imposed on Africans in urban areas. Under the 1920 Masters and Servants Proclamation corporal punishment could be meted out to servants for desertion or disobedience; the Vagrancy Proclamation of the same

General Smuts (right) receives the German surrender

year empowered the authorities to imprison or fine Africans not in officially approved employment or housing. The Native Administration Proclamation of 1922 replaced German controls with South African 'pass laws', forcing Africans over the age of 14 to carry identity documents in the Police Zone and restricting their movement.[15]

South African colonists, like the Germans they had replaced, regarded the land as theirs for settlement and the black population as 'labour units'. The annual report of the Union of South Africa on the administration of the territory proclaimed in 1920: 'The native question . . . is synonymous with the Labour question.'

In South African statements to the Permanent Mandates Commission, the objectives of their policy with regard to the black population were revealed. The dog tax, they admitted, was 'designed partly to compel [Africans] to come out to work'; Africans were only permitted in urban areas so long as their numbers did not surpass 'the bare requirements of urban employers'; 'grazing fees . . . compelled [Africans] to obtain cash to meet the fees . . . by working'.

Steps were taken to ensure that all African men of working age in the Police Zone would be forced into waged labour. According to the *Annual Report* of 1920, 'able bodied men' should not be allowed to live in the 'reserves', which should only be for 'the old and infirm'. Grazing fees were imposed to prevent Africans owning large herds.[16]

Penalties for certain crimes were deliberately stiffened to provide more prison labourers, who were forced to work without pay. On white farms, many workers still lived in conditions of semi-slavery and received no cash wages. Child labour began to be used on farms – by 1954 one out of every four contracted farm workers was under the age of 16.[17]

RESISTANCE CONTINUES

To increase the supply of migrant labour from the populous regions north of the Police Zone, the South African authorities pressurised chiefs and kings into co-operating in recruitment. Recalcitrant leaders were overthrown by military force and replaced. Missionaries were required to urge 'all natives under their influence to seek employment'.[18] In 1917, a military force was dispatched against King Mandume of the Kwanyama, who was resisting both South African colonialism to the south of his territory and Portuguese rule to the north in Angola. Mandume and a hundred of his followers were killed after a joint South African-Portuguese offensive. After his defeat, the South African authorities stated: 'Our representatives in Ovamboland will continue to watch the situation closely and do all in their power to induce the able-bodied men of the different tribes to go south to engage themselves as labourers on the railways, mines and farms . . .'[19]

In 1932 the South African authorities again intervened militarily in the north, overthrowing Chief Ipumbu of the Ukuambi.

Resistance to South African colonialism also continued in the south. The Bondelswarts, who had been confined to a small arid reserve and had been reduced to virtual starvation by taxes and stock controls, resisted the arrest of their leaders in 1922. The South African army, air force and police bombed and machine-gunned their defensive position on a hill, indiscriminately killing over one hundred men, women and children.

Two years later the army was used against the Rehoboth community, who had negotiated limited self-government for a small republic they had established in central Namibia before German colonisation. In response to Rehoboth agitation for full independence, the main town was surrounded. Over 600

King Mandume

Rehobothers, together with Herero and Nama supporters, were arrested. Afterwards, the Rehoboth Council was stripped of its powers.[20]

The continuing resistance of separate communities was paralleled by the formation of the first African nationalist organisations and trade unions.

Branches of the Universal Negro Improvement Association of Marcus Garvey were established in Windhoek and Luderitz in the 1920s, and several hundred members were signed up. The South African based Industrial and Commercial Workers Union (ICU), the first mass non-racial trade union, took root in Luderitz, while contract workers from the north formed benefit societies which laid the foundation for future worker organisations.[21]

'CREEPING ANNEXATION'

By 1943 a white legislature, which had been established in Namibia in 1925, was pressing for the territory to be annexed by South Africa. When the United Nations was established at the end of the Second World War, General Smuts, the South African Prime Minister, argued that Namibia should be incorporated into South Africa. The UN refused the South African demand, stating that the League of Nations mandate remained valid. It requested South Africa to place Namibia under trusteeship, as had been done with the other mandated territories.[22]

For fourteen years Pretoria resisted all pressures from the UN General Assembly to administer Namibia in terms of its mandate – even after the International Court of Justice (ICJ) had ruled that it should. The National Party government which came to power in 1948 took a more defiant attitude than Smuts, refusing to provide annual reports on its administration to the UN and giving white settlers the right to elect MPs to the South African parliament.[23].

Segregation and discrimination were intensified inside Namibia through efforts by the National Party government to extend the South African apartheid system to the territory. In 1964 the government's Odendaal Commission drew up a blueprint for the division of the black population into 11 separate 'population groups' and the establishment, on the basis of the old reserves, of 10 'homelands' or bantustans. This was designed to leave the whites in full control of the bulk of the territory.[24]

NATIONAL AND INTERNATIONAL RESISTANCE

South Africa's 'creeping annexation' was opposed by Namibians. African leaders sent messages to the UN detailing oppressive conditions and demanding that their country be granted its independence or placed under international control. They were prevented from leaving the territory, but dispatched Michael Scott, an Anglican clergyman serving in South Africa, to petition the UN.

In the 1950s the first Namibian representatives were able to speak to the UN and messages were smuggled out of the country by Andimba Toivo ja Toivo and other young leaders. In 1960 alone the UN received 120 messages and petitions.[25]

To oppose apartheid and to agitate for independence, Namibians formed a number of political, cultural and student organisations, including the Ovamboland People's Organisation (OPO), which in 1960 was transformed into a fully fledged nationalist movement, SWAPO.

Membership of OPO grew rapidly when it launched a campaign against the contract labour system in 1959. OPO and other Namibian organisations also campaigned against the new bantustan authorities and in Windhoek there were protests and boycotts against the forced removal of the African population to the segregated township of Katutura, further from the town centre. These protests were forcefully broken up by the police, who opened fire on demonstrators on 10 December 1959, killing at least 11 people.[26]

This atrocity was a turning point in the Namibian independence struggle, galvanising the Namibian people into a wider unity and more militant action. In the face of continuing South African repression, SWAPO leaders like Sam Nujoma left the country to build an external base for the liberation movement and to prepare for an armed struggle.

Namibians were supported in their resistance to South Africa by fellow Africans – initially the African National Congress (ANC) of South Africa and Chief Tshekedi of Botswana, later by the newly independent African states. In 1960, in an effort to add teeth to UN demands, the Governments of Liberia and Ethiopia took the issue of Namibia to the ICJ. They charged South Africa with failure to meet its mandate obligations.[27]

After six years of argument the Court concluded that the two countries had no legal basis to bring the case, and declined to rule on the issue.[28]

The response of the exiled SWAPO leadership to the ICJ's failure in July 1966 to deliver a judgement was straightforward: 'We have no alternative but to rise in arms and bring about our liberation.' The first clashes between SWAPO guerrillas and South African police took place a month later at Omgulumbashe in northern Namibia (*see Chapter 8*). [29]

Forced removal

THE MANDATE REVOKED

The UN General Assembly, strengthened in its opposition to colonialism by the new membership of dozens of African and Asian states, also responded swiftly to the ICJ's failure to make a ruling. In October 1966 it passed a resolution terminating South Africa's mandate on the grounds that it had violated its provisions by imposing apartheid and repressing the people. It ordered the South African administration out of the territory and placed Namibia under direct UN responsibility until its independence. The General Assembly acted in terms of the powers it inherited from the Council of the League of Nations.[30]

To administer Namibia and to prepare it for nationhood, the UN General Assembly established the Council for Namibia at its headquarters in New York. The Council, composed of member states, was charged with administering the affairs of Namibia until independence. It would mobilise international support for the Namibian independence struggle and work to ensure that UN members adhered to resolutions on Namibia. It would also represent Namibian interests in international organisations, issue travel documents and fund programmes to train and educate Namibians. The UN Institute for Namibia was established in Lusaka as an educational college.[31]

In 1969 the UN Security Council affirmed the termination of South Africa's mandate and demanded its withdrawal from Namibia. In June 1971 the ICJ confirmed the UN's direct responsibility for Namibia. It also confirmed that South Africa's presence in Namibia was illegal and that it was obliged to end its occupation of the territory. It stated that UN member states should refrain from any acts which would imply recognition of South Africa's administration or presence in Namibia.[32]

The decision precipitated mass resistance inside Namibia, leading to a general strike of contract workers at the end of 1971, and subsequent peasant uprisings in the north. This marked a new phase in the liberation struggle.

The court is of opinion . . .

(1) that, the continued presence of South Africa in Namibia being illegal, South Africa is under obligation to withdraw its administration from Namibia immediately and thus put an end to its occupation of the Territory . . .

(2) that States Members of the United Nations are under obligation to recognise the illegality of South Africa's presence in Namibia and the invalidity of its acts on behalf of or concerning Namibia, and to refrain from any acts and in particular any dealings with the Government of South Africa implying recognition of the legality of, or lending support or assistance to, such presence and administration . . .

(3) that it is incumbent upon States which are not Members of the United Nations to give assistance, within the scope of subparagraph (2) above, in the action which has been taken by the United Nations with regard to Namibia.

Extract from the Advisory Opinion of the International Court of Justice, 21 June 1971

International Court of Justice in session, 1971

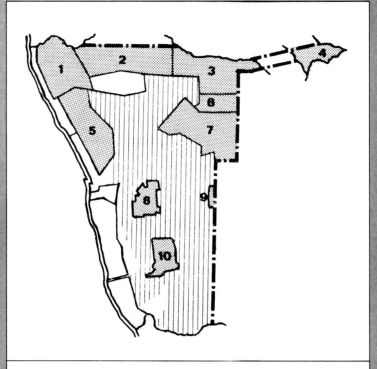

Namibia segregated

□ — Bantustans:

|||| — White farmland

□ — Government land

1. Kaokoland
2. Ovambo
3. Kavango
4. East Caprivi
5. Damaraland

6. Bushmanland
7. Hereroland
8. Rehoboth
9. Tswanaland
10. Namaland

2 THE APARTHEID COLONY

Many characteristics of nineteeth-century colonialism persist in Namibia under South African occupation. The apartheid system overlays and reinforces the colonial pattern of white domination.

Imposed by violence, apartheid is maintained through force reinforced by legal, social and economic measures.

Apartheid divides the entire population according to colour. The black population is further divided into 11 separate groups mainly on the basis of language while whites speaking different languages are formed into one group and given decisive control.[1]

LAND

Control of the land, especially farm land and land bearing minerals, has preoccupied the colonial rulers of Namibia. The forceful seizure of land underpinned white settlement and the South African government continuously extended the area set aside for white farmers, almost doubling it between 1925 and 1962. Africans were forced to live in only about 10 per cent of the Police Zone, in reserves which were mostly on the desert margins. Thousands of Namibians were forcibly removed and resettled. Only in the north were Africans able to retain some control over their land, but even these rights were steadily eroded.[2]

The unequal division of land was formalised by the Odendaal Commission which made recommendations to the South African Government in 1964. The commission called for the division of the country into a white section and 10 black 'homelands', also known as bantustans. The white section, based on the old German Police Zone, would consist of more than 60 per cent of the territory, including the commercial farming and mining areas. Apart from securing white control over most of Namibia, the bantustan system was aimed at undermining the national liberation struggle by dividing the oppressed population.

Extending the colonial policy of African 'reserves', apartheid ideology called for the establishment of a bantustan for each 'population group'. Three new bantustans would be established in remote areas, even though in each case only between 4 and 13 per cent of the designated 'population group' lived there. Full implementation of the Odendaal Commission's recommendations would have meant the removal and resettlement of nearly one third of the black population.[3]

The Odendaal plan almost doubled the area of Namibia reserved for blacks – but it removed Africans from some of the best farmland and apportioned them large tracts of sandy desert or barren mountains. The

Damaraland bantustan

Herero, for example, were forced into the barren Kalahari sands in which so many had perished during the German genocide. The apartheid population division, and the bantustans to which each group was allocated, bore little resemblance to the traditional polities of Namibian society.[4]

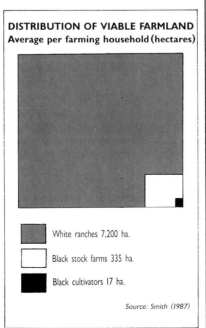

DISTRIBUTION OF VIABLE FARMLAND
Average per farming household (hectares)

White ranches 7,200 ha.

Black stock farms 335 ha.

Black cultivators 17 ha.

Source: Smith (1987)

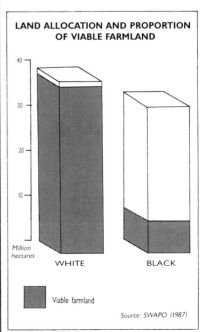

LAND ALLOCATION AND PROPORTION OF VIABLE FARMLAND

Million hectares

WHITE   BLACK

Viable farmland

Source: SWAPO (1987)

19

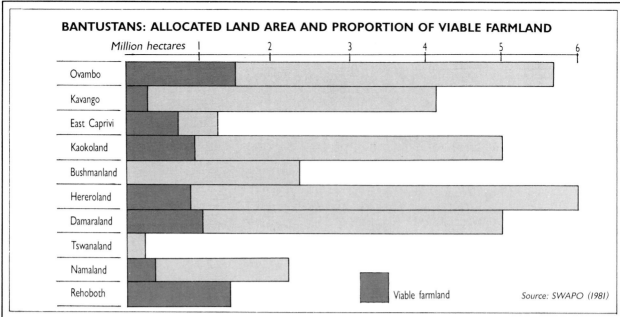

BANTUSTANS: ALLOCATED LAND AREA AND PROPORTION OF VIABLE FARMLAND

Million hectares

	1	2	3	4	5	6
Ovambo						
Kavango						
East Caprivi						
Kaokoland						
Bushmanland						
Hereroland						
Damaraland						
Tswanaland						
Namaland						
Rehoboth						

Viable farmland

Source: SWAPO (1981)

DIVISION OF THE POPULATION

In terms of the 1970 Identity Documents in South West Africa Act all Namibians are identified as belonging to one of the 12 designated 'population groups' (*see table*). Children are usually registered at birth as belonging to one of these groups, and are required by law to be classified at the age of 16.[5]

The criteria for these divisions may involve physical appearance, language, parentage or place of residence. The South African regime claims that the divisions it has imposed on the population are historical and geographical and reflect the different cultures and languages in Namibia. However, the distinctions are in many cases spurious, while other differences are ignored. New classifications, such as 'Caprivians' and 'Kaokolanders' were created for the purposes of setting up bantustans, ignoring historic and language differences. A category of 'Coloureds' was devised to accommodate mainly people who could not be classified into other 'groups'. No historical or geographical group distinctions are made between people classified as white although there are distinct language and cultural differences between the German, English and Afrikaans-speaking groups.

APARTHEID DIVISION OF THE POPULATION
ACCORDING TO THE 1981 CENSUS

POPULATION GROUP	NUMBERS
Black:	810 579
Wambo	505 774
Kavango	94 640
Herero	76 293
Damara	76 169
Caprivi	38 594
Tswana	6 706
Other	12 403
Brown:	115 961
Nama	48 539
Coloureds	42 241
Rehoboth Basters	25 181
White	75 946
Bushmen	29 441
TOTAL:	1 031 927

Source: Directorate for Development Co-ordination Windhoek.
Figures exclude Walvis Bay.

More than 13 main languages are spoken in Namibia – approximately half the population speak Oshivambo languages as a mother tongue. The languages spoken originally by whites – German, English and Afrikaans – are used officially by the central administration. Afrikaans is most commonly used in the workplace. English is preferred by the liberation movement and, in order to gain international access, an increasing number of Namibians are adopting English.

According to the 1981 census, the population of Namibia was slightly over 1 million.[6] However, given that only about one in four births is registered and a complete census has not been carried out by the authorities, UN experts regard this figure as being deliberately calculated at a low level for South Africa's political purposes. By 1985 the estimated population had grown to over 1 and a ½ million.[7]

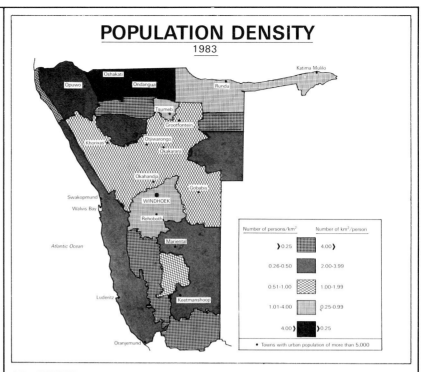

POPULATION DENSITY
1983

Number of persons/km²		Number of km²/person	
> 0.25		4.00 >	
0.26-0.50		2.00-3.99	
0.51-1.00		1.00-1.99	
1.01-4.00		0.25-0.99	
4.00 >		> 0.25	

• Towns with urban population of more than 5,000

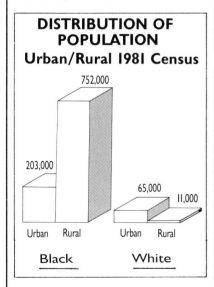

DISTRIBUTION OF POPULATION
Urban/Rural 1981 Census

	Black		White	
	Urban	Rural	Urban	Rural
	203,000	752,000	65,000	11,000

The white population is more likely to be accurately measured. It was given as 76,000 in the 1981 census – in 1985 it was estimated at 85,000.[8] The number of whites in Namibia declined markedly during the 1970s, largely as a result of South African settlers and civil servants returning to South Africa in the face of political uncertainty and the decline of the Namibian economy.

SETTLEMENT

Estimates show that by far the most densely populated rural areas of Namibia are in the northern bantustans, particularly in Ovambo which alone accommodates about 44 per cent of the total population, most of whom live in widely dispersed homesteads. More recently tens of thousands of people have settled in informal squatter communities around the two main urban centres in the north, Ondangua-Oluno and Oshakati. Many of them have deserted the rural areas because of drought, South African military campaigns and the abolition of 'influx controls, on the black population in 1977' (see Chapter 3).[9]

Parts of the other northern bantustans, notably the eastern Caprivi and areas bordering the Kavango river are densely settled. Much of the countryside in the south and central parts consists of large white ranches, infertile bantustan areas or government-controlled land, much of which is used for tourism. This includes the coastal desert strip in which diamonds are mined, parts of which are restricted.

About a quarter of the total population is urbanised, with over 100,000 people concentrated in the capital, Windhoek. Eighty-five per cent of whites live in urban areas.[10]

Urban areas are segregated. Whites live in the central and suburban areas and black people are forced to live in crowded townships on the outskirts.

Residential segregation and the exclusion of Africans from the centres of towns was enforced through the Native (Urban Areas) Proclamation 1951 and through restrictive clauses in title deeds. Africans were prohibited from being in urban areas for more than 72 hours without a permit and could be banished to the bantustans if their labour was not required.[11]

Separate townships, such as Katutura and Khomasdal in Windhoek, were established for people classified as African and Coloured respectively. Katutura was further zoned into 'population group' areas.

Khomasdal and Katutura together house roughly twice the number of people who live in the areas of Windhoek which were zoned for whites, where almost all facilities are situated.[12]

Pressure on the limited land resources available to black Namibians, coupled with a relaxation of the pass laws in 1977, has resulted in greatly accelerated rural-urban migration in recent years. The authorities have been unwilling to increase the housing stock, with the result that large unofficial shanty settlements have sprung up near major urban centres.

SEPARATE AMENITIES

The apartheid division of Namibia into black and white zones, and the further segregation into 'population groups', has been accompanied by social, legal, educational, sporting and cultural segregation. Much of South Africa's apartheid legislation was extended to Namibia, sometimes in modified form.[13]

The 1934 Immorality Proclamation and the 1953 Mixed Marriages Ordinance prohibited sex across apartheid barriers, while other laws and regulations established segregated civic amenities, places of entertainment, toilets, transport, sports facilities, cultural amenities, restaurants – virtually all aspects of life were affected.

Since the late 1970s, largely as a result of South African efforts to promote a collaborative elite and inject credibility into client administrations, many of these laws have been repealed. However, the basic pattern of segregation and white domination has been retained as a result of underlying economic and educational discrimination, the bantustan system, and white control over most economic, administrative, educational and social facilities.

Blacks are now legally entitled to eat in formerly whites-only restaurants, patronise cinemas and sports events and rent or buy houses in the areas previously reserved exclusively for whites. In practice, however, segregation has remained and in many areas, particularly in smaller towns, black Namibians who attempt to use facilities are subjected to

Makeshift homes in Gibeon, Namaland bantustan

abuse or physical attack. Many people cannot afford to patronise cinemas, municipal swimming pools and other facilities and lack transport to these places which are generally not situated in black residential areas.[14]

Schools and some school sports remain segregated and many health facilities have retained 'whites only' policies. Many of these facilities are controlled by the powerful Administration for Whites (*see below, 'Bantustans and Second-Tier Administrations'*). Residential desegregation has only affected a small elite, mainly teachers, nurses and civil servants, who have been able to afford higher land and house prices by taking out government loans.[15]

CENTRAL AUTHORITY

For over a century, Namibia has been administered along colonial lines, first from Germany and then from South Africa. Control of the territory is in the hands of the South African Government, although this is illegal under international law.

The South African parliament has passed specific laws for Namibia, as well as extending much South African legislation to the territory. Further laws and regulations have been introduced by proclamation by the South African State President,

acting through the senior administrator for the territory. Many of the most important South African laws relating to the control of black South Africans were extended to Namibia in this way.[16]

Strategic decisions about Namibia are today taken mainly by the South African State Security Council rather than parliament. The council is strongly influenced by military and police commanders. The South African Defence Force (SADF) itself plays an increasingly important role in formulating policy and in the administration of the territory, especially in the war zones.[17]

While final control rests in Pretoria, local Namibian officials collaborating with the South African occupation have been given varying degrees of power. This is a result mainly of South African efforts to build an alternative to SWAPO and to undercut UN independence plans by preparing the territory for 'unilateral independence'. However, local officials have always been prevented from gaining control over the military and police forces, conducting foreign affairs or exercising significant economic powers.

After 1977 most South African government departments in Namibia were gradually transferred to the authority of the South African Administrator-General in Windhoek, with the exceptions of finance, foreign affairs and the police and army.

The 1980 Government Service Act established a Namibian civil service and various administrative departments, including a South West Africa Territory Force (SWATF) and police force (SWAPOL). However, these were merely administrative structures and effective control over all police and military forces in the territory remains with the SADF and South African Police.[18].

In 1978 the South African government held carefully controlled elections to a 'national assembly' in Windhoek. These were boycotted by SWAPO, which viewed them as an attempt to undercut the UN demand for internationally supervised elections leading to independence. The boycott was widely supported and backed by the churches. Most of the SWAPO leadership was detained, and voting took place under martial-law conditions in many parts of the country. The Democratic Turnhalle Alliance (DTA), backed by Pretoria and based almost entirely on parties participating in the bantustan system, was declared winner of the election.[19]

No government in the world recognised the DTA administration and it failed to gain credibility as an alternative to SWAPO, despite massive South African financial and military support. Weakened by internal splits and defections and undermined by corruption and inefficiency, it was abolished by Pretoria early in 1983. The territory was then ruled directly by the Administrator-General, acting on orders from Pretoria.[20]

To replace the DTA administration the South African regime entered into discussions with a number of small parties in Namibia including bantustan groups and political parties representing the whites. Some of these groups came together in the Multi-Party Conference (MPC) and in June 1985 the MPC was installed as a new administration in Windhoek, called the Transitional Government of National Unity (TGNU).[21]

This time, the South African Government made no attempt to stage its own elections. Members of the new 'National Assembly' and 'Cabinet' were simply appointed by Pretoria on a proportional basis from the seven political groups participating in the MPC. The new administration was given greater powers than its DTA predecessor, but the conduct of the war, foreign affairs and overall control of the economy remained with Pretoria. A Constitutional Council chaired by a South African judge was established to draw up a constitution for a nominally independent state.[22]

Once again, no state in the world would recognise Pretoria's new administration but steps were taken to give the impression that the administration was preparing the territory for independence. This included the release of many SWAPO leaders who had been imprisoned since the 1960s.

As a client of Pretoria, the MPC could not deal with the fundamental economic and political inequalities in the territory. At the same time, it was seen as being partly responsible for increased repression inside Namibia and continuing delay in the implementation of the UN plan for independence. It failed to expand its very limited base of support in the territory and an 'independence' constitution it produced after 18 months of wrangling was rejected by Pretoria. In spite of severe repression, SWAPO dramatically increased both its political mobilisation of the Namibian people and its armed struggle after the MPC administration was established.[23]

BANTUSTANS AND SECOND TIER ADMINISTRATIONS

The government-commissioned Odendaal report of 1964 set the framework for the Namibian bantustan structure which was transformed in the DTA period into a 'second-tier' of 'ethnic administrations'.

Most of the second-tier administrations are weak and have

Protest against the South African Multi-Party Conference administration

little influence, but the Administration for Whites, which is dominated by the National Party, controls many of the territory's resources, including the white schools and health facilities and much of the country's agriculture. It is far wealthier than the other administrations as taxes levied on the wealthy white section of the population accrue directly to it.

Before the Odendaal Report, control over the African population was vested in the South African State President, who was empowered to rule by proclamation. Later, powers were delegated to the Minister of Bantu Administration and Development.

Odendaal's recommendations resulted in the Development of Self-Government for Native Nations in South West Africa Act of 1968 and later amendments. These laws provided for the establishment of bantustans on the basis of the northern 'reserves' and for other bantustans to be set up through population removals and the transfer of land. Legislative councils with limited powers could be established.

The powers of the bantustan legislatures were increased in 1972 and the following year provision was made for them to become 'self-governing'. This included the paraphernalia of 'independence' such as a flag and anthem, as well as powers to levy taxes and establish courts where punishments including floggings could be meted out.[24]

Members of the legislatures were drawn mainly from officially recognised 'headmen' and paid chiefs. Many of these were imposed by the South African regime, which had systematically removed and replaced traditional leaders who refused to collaborate. South African civil servants were seconded to the bantustans and effectively ran most of the administrations.

By the end of 1976 bantustan councils had been established in

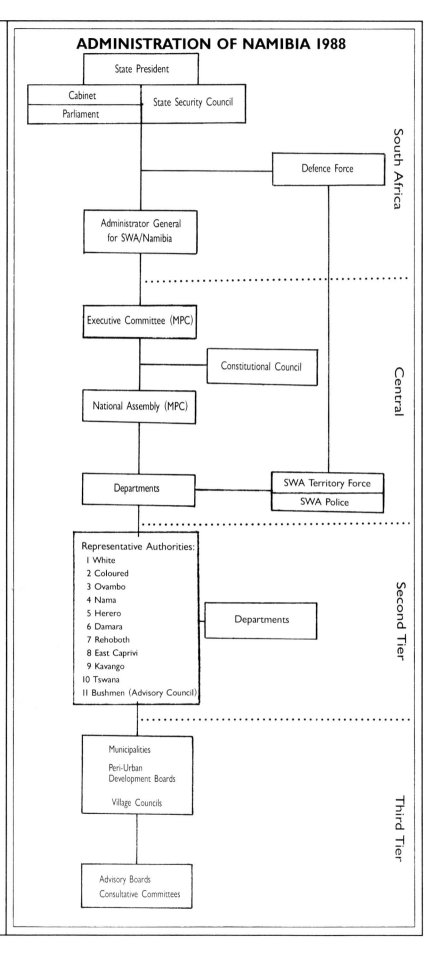

ADMINISTRATION OF NAMIBIA 1988

State President
Cabinet
Parliament
State Security Council
Defence Force
Administrator General for SWA/Namibia

South Africa

Executive Committee (MPC)
Constitutional Council
National Assembly (MPC)
Departments
SWA Territory Force
SWA Police

Central

Representative Authorities:
1 White
2 Coloured
3 Ovambo
4 Nama
5 Herero
6 Damara
7 Rehoboth
8 East Caprivi
9 Kavango
10 Tswana
11 Bushmen (Advisory Council)

Departments

Second Tier

Municipalities
Peri-Urban Development Boards
Village Councils

Advisory Boards
Consultative Committees

Third Tier

Ovambo, Kavango and East Caprivi. Rehoboth, which had been independent in the early period of colonial rule, had also been made 'self-governing', and a Coloured Council had been appointed to deal with people classified into that group. In the remaining bantustans administration was conducted through 'headmen' and 'advisory' structures. A Legislative Assembly elected by whites exercised effective control over most of the rest of the country, although it was subordinate to the South African parliament.[25]

Bantustan military units were recruited in many areas, but authority over these remained with the SADF. With locally recruited police, the troops were used to protect the bantustan authorities, who relied on force to maintain control. Popular opposition to the bantustan scheme was reflected most graphically in 1973 when, in response to a SWAPO call, 98 per cent of people eligible to vote for a limited number of elected positions on the Ovambo bantustan council boycotted the election.[26]

By the mid-1970s South African strategy for continued colonial control had shifted from preparing each of the bantustans for 'independence' to pushing the territory as a whole into 'independence', whilst maintaining the second-tier administrations.

In 1980, after the DTA had been installed in the central administration, the bantustan administrative structures, as well as the white Legislative Assembly and the Coloured Council, were reconstituted as second-tier Representative Authorities. However, the structure set up to deal with people classified as 'Bushmen' was excluded – making 10 authorities in all.[27]

The powers of the Representative Authorities were set out in Proclamation AG8 of 1980. This gave them authority over land tenure, farming, schools, health services, welfare, pensions, some of the courts, culture and some taxation. These powers were not restricted to geographic areas but covered all individuals classified as members of that population group. The effect was to entrench segregation, inequality and white control, and to further fragment the country.[28]

Elections were held for some posts in five of the legislative authorities in November 1980 – in other cases officials were simply retained or appointed.

The system of second-tier authorities, with its multiple health, education and other departments, has generated considerable confusion and wastage. Patronage and corruption has become endemic and a large, unwieldy bureaucracy has grown as Pretoria has attempted to buy allegiance – one out of every 29 Namibians is employed by the state.[29]

Many of the administrations, situated in remote towns or villages in or near the bantustans, lack resources, while the Administration for Whites has had at its disposal almost double the funds of all the other authorities combined. With control over many schools, health facilities and other amenities, and its extensive budget, the Administration for Whites is in many ways more powerful than the central authority and has effectively been able to exercise a veto over the central administration.[30]

Most of the second-tier authorities are controlled by small parties which are based amongst those who collaborate with the apartheid regime. Their legislative power is limited and they rely for funds on the central administration, which in turn is largely dependent on subsidies from Pretoria.

LOCAL AUTHORITIES

Black Namibians are also denied power in local municipal authorities. White voters elect Municipal Councils in Windhoek and the larger towns. Peri-Urban Development Boards and Village Management Boards in smaller centres are also controlled by white officials.[31]

In black townships, Advisory Boards and Consultative Committees have been established. These are usually composed of appointed members, have no administrative or financial powers, and can only make recommendations to the white local authorities. Urban areas in bantustans are administered by the second-tier authorities.[32]

3 ECONOMIC EXPLOITATION

Extremes of wealth and poverty abound in Namibia. Wages for whites are estimated to be 18 times greater than those of blacks, and the poorest 40 per cent of the population receive only about 6 or 7 per cent of total income.[1]. According to recent surveys, between 80 and 90 per cent of black households in urban areas live on or below the minimum subsistence level; people in the bantustans and rural areas face even worse poverty especially during drought and in war-affected areas.

The profitability of South African and transnational companies and the prosperity of white farmers, businessmen and professionals depends on the exploitation of black labour, in particular through the migrant-labour system. Founded on the German forced-labour regime and developed through the imposition of apartheid, South African control over black labour has rested on the bantustan system, segregation, discrimination and the suppression of workers' political and trade-union activities.

Africans are forced into migrant labour through the shortage of land and lack of employment in the bantustans, which act as reservoirs of labour. More than two-thirds of the black population live in the bantustans, which have been systematically underdeveloped, denied investment and markets and overcrowded as a result of population controls and removals.

Only about 170,000 out of a total estimated work-force of over 600,000 were estimated to be in paid employment in 1986. An estimated half of the economically active population are engaged in subsistence agriculture in the bantustans which cannot sustain the number of people living in them. The vast

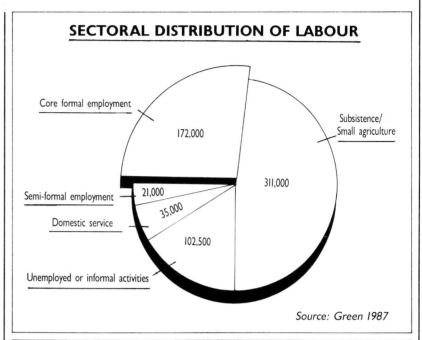

SECTORAL DISTRIBUTION OF LABOUR

Core formal employment — 172,000
Subsistence/Small agriculture — 311,000
Semi-formal employment — 21,000
Domestic service — 35,000
Unemployed or informal activities — 102,500

Source: Green 1987

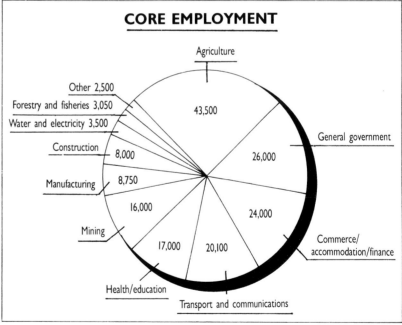

CORE EMPLOYMENT

Agriculture — 43,500
Other 2,500
Forestry and fisheries 3,050
Water and electricity 3,500
Construction — 8,000
Manufacturing — 8,750
Mining — 16,000
Health/education — 17,000
Transport and communications — 20,100
Commerce/accommodation/finance — 24,000
General government — 26,000

majority of Africans in waged employment work as unskilled labourers, mostly on a migrant basis. A study published in 1984 showed that only 1.5 per cent of African workers and 8 per cent of Coloured workers were employed in white-collar jobs. Urban unemployment and rural underemployment for blacks is extremely high, but few whites are unemployed.[2]

An estimated 60 per cent of black Namibian workers are involved with subsistence agriculture in the bantustans. Women are estimated to make up about a third of black Namibians in waged employment, but eight out of ten of these women work as domestic servants for minimal wages.[3].

The Namibian economy reflects the imbalances of colonial exploitation. Whites earn roughly 17.5 times as much per person of the gross domestic product (GDP) as blacks. There is little correlation between what is produced and what is needed in the country. Most goods produced for cash are exported; 85 per cent of goods consumed, including more than half the foodstuffs, are imported. Primary products – mostly minerals or lightly processed commodities – make up the bulk of exports. There is virtually no manufacturing base.[4]

NAMIBIA: EXPORTS 1983
Rand Millions

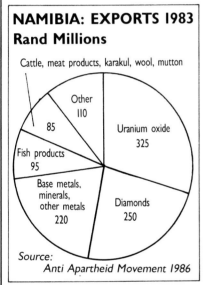

Cattle, meat products, karakul, wool, mutton

Other 110
85
Fish products 95
Base metals, minerals, other metals 220
Uranium oxide 325
Diamonds 250

Source:
Anti Apartheid Movement 1986

NAMIBIA: IMPORTS 1983
Rand Millions

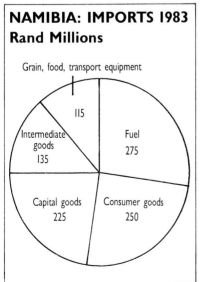

Grain, food, transport equipment

115
Intermediate goods 135
Fuel 275
Capital goods 225
Consumer goods 250

The transnational-controlled mining industry is the most significant earner of foreign exchange and makes up about a quarter of GDP. The South African-based Anglo-American Corporation, which dominates mining, is by far the most important private-sector force in Namibia's economy.[5]

Three out of every five economically active Namibians are engaged in agriculture, but much of this is subsistence farming and it contributes only about 5 per cent of GDP. The once-significant fishing industry, which is also dominated by South African and overseas interests, has been severely eroded by overfishing.[6]

Much of the wealth produced in Namibia has left the country. Up to 20 per cent of GDP is estimated to have been removed annually as profits and dividends, and there has been little re-investment.[7]

In the mid-1970s, after a sustained boom which saw vast profits being accumulated by transnational and South African investors and growing prosperity for white settlers, the Namibian economy went into decline. This was the result of drought, a world drop in mineral prices, economic mismanagement, the depletion of resources and lack of productive investment due

DISTRIBUTION OF NAMIBIA'S GDP 1983

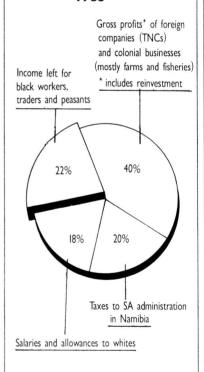

Income left for black workers, traders and peasants

Gross profits* of foreign companies (TNCs) and colonial businesses (mostly farms and fisheries)
* includes reinvestment

22%
40%
18%
20%

Taxes to SA administration in Namibia

Salaries and allowances to whites

Source: Smith 1986

largely to the escalating war between the South African occupation forces and the People's Liberation Army of Namibia (PLAN).

STRUCTURE OF THE ECONOMY 1985
GDP by kind of economic activity
(Rand Millions)

Mining: 908
Government: 470
Commerce: 283
Finance: 176
Agriculture: 156
Transport: 144
Manufacturing: 113
Other: 262

Source: Statistical/Economic Review 1987
Department of Finance, Windhoek

All economic dealings with South Africa's occupation of Namibia are illegal in international law. In an effort to preserve wealth belonging to a free and independent Namibia, the exploitation of Namibia's natural resources has been specifically declared illegal by the UN. In 1974 the Council for Namibia enacted Decree No. 1 for the Protection of the Natural Resources of Namibia, which prohibited the export of Namibian goods without UN permission. This and other UN measures have however been largely ignored by South African and transnational corporations.

DECREE No. 1 (Extract)
No person or entity, whether a body corporate or unincorporated, may search for, prospect for, explore for, take, extract, mine, process, refine, use, sell, export, or distribute any natural resource, whether animal or mineral, situated or found to be situated within the territorial limits of Namibia without the consent and permission of the United Nations Council for Namibia or any person authorised to act on its behalf for the purpose of giving such permission or such consent.

United Nations Council for Namibia Decree No. 1 for the Protection of the Natural Resources of Namibia, 27.9.74

With the exception of manufacturing and the service and transport industries, there were dramatic falls in production in all sectors of the economy after 1976, although by 1986 a few sectors showed a limited recovery. At the same time administrative bureaucracies mushroomed as the South African regime pushed ahead with its bantustan policies and set up a surrogate administration.

The occupation of Namibia is estimated to cost Pretoria upwards of R3,000 million a year, mostly in military and administrative costs. This expenditure is offset by profits from South African companies operating in Namibia, the processing and use of Namibian goods and materials in South Africa and Namibia's role as a market for South African exports.[8]

The South African regime has also, through international borrowing to finance its occupation of Namibia, incurred an external debt which by one calculation in 1986 could have been equal to its total annual export earnings. This debt could cripple an independent Namibia but in international law an independent government would have no obligation to meet it.[9]

Walvis Bay

Mining

Although it is by far the most important source of wealth in the territory, the mining industry employs only 5 per cent of waged workers in Namibia.[10]

The diamond fields at Oranjemund in the extreme south of the country, which are controlled by Consolidated Diamond Mines (CDM), a subsidiary of Anglo-American's De Beers conglomerate, are the territory's single most important economic asset. At present the diamonds are marketed through De Beers' Central Selling Organisation in London and sent to cutting centres in New York, Tel Aviv, Antwerp and other cities.

Diamond resources have been seriously denuded by CDM's efforts to extract the maximum possible profit from the diamond fields without regard to their long-term viability. Evidence to a South African-appointed commission of inquiry indicated that the diamond fields might be made unprofitable by 1991 as a result of overmining.[11]

Uranium mining is second in importance to diamond mining. Uranium ore is extracted from the Rossing mine near Swakopmund, established in the 1970s by the British-based transnational corporation Rio-Tinto Zinc (RTZ) with investment and long-term supply contracts from major nuclear corporations in other Western countries.

Base metals, chiefly copper, lead and zinc, constitute the remaining important mining activities. Seventy per cent of this mining is controlled by Tsumeb Corporation Limited (TCL), which is controlled by Anglo-American and the British-based company Consolidated Goldfields through Goldfields of South Africa.[12]

Other minerals from TCL, such as gold, silver, cadmium and germanium, as well as tin, vanadium and lithium from other foreign-owned mines, ensure that mineral exports are

Tsumeb copper mine

by far the largest source of foreign currency. However, much revenue is lost owing to lack of government control.

The Namibian mines have played a principal role in the development of the system of contract labour. Migrant labourers form the bulk of the black mine work-force, although at some of the larger complexes a minority of black workers are now housed in family accommodation.

The major mining companies claim to operate non-racial wage scales, but the vast majority of black workers are employed at the lower rates. At Rossing, black workers constituted only 3 per cent of those in professional grades and 12 per cent of those in skilled grades in 1983 – the position at other mines was similar or worse. In 1987 it was reported that white miners earned on average 24 times more than their black colleagues.[13]

BREAKDOWN OF TOTAL SALES INCOME (MINERALS) 1982/3

Wages of black workers — 10%
Cost of inputs — 30%
Profit and taxes — 37%
Depreciation — 6%
Whites' salaries — 17%

Source: Smith 1986

Exploration for oil has concentrated on the Kudu natural gas field off the southern Namibian coast. However, exoloitation would involve considerable investment and would entail a further violation of Decree No. 1 by foreign companies. Exploration of this potentially rich resource has been overseen by the South African oil parastatal, Soekor, and it is said that the field could supply a third of South African fuel requirements.[14]

Fishing

Namibia's rich resources of fish off the Atlantic coast, potentially a larger currency-earner than diamonds, have been systematically exploited by South African boats operating in inshore waters and by other foreign fleets in offshore waters. In the late 1970s the inshore industry all but collapsed as a result of the exhaustion of fish stocks and revenue cannot be obtained from offshore catches because Pretoria cannot claim legal title to a 200-mile zone. Fish processing plants, mainly at Walvis Bay, were closed and hundreds of workers dismissed although there was a limited revival in the 1980s.

Agriculture

Farming in Namibia reflects the division of the land into, on the one hand, the impoverished bantustans where communal subsistence farming takes place and, on the other, the rich white ranching and crop-growing areas.

African agriculture and animal husbandry have been undermined by the expropriation of land, the channelling of funds and expertise only to white farmers, the manipulation of markets and the removal of large numbers of people to the bantustans. Agriculture has also been disrupted by the war as South African armoured vehicles have destroyed crops and fences and people have left their homes to escape army terror or to join the fighting forces of SWAPO.

In the north, which was once self-sufficient in food, production of the staple crop, *mahangu* millet, has declined rapidly. By 1974 at least a third of all cash expenditure in the Ovambo bantustan went towards the purchase of food.[15]

With rare exceptions, commercial farms are owned and controlled by fewer than 4,000 whites, who have been granted possession of 80 per cent of the stock-raising land. The farms were built up on the basis of cheap black labour and government loans, subsidies and controls of the market.

A meat-processing industry has been established on the basis of cattle ranching, although two-thirds of the cattle are sent to South Africa for slaughter, depriving Namibia of income. In the south farmers raise karakul (Persian) lambs for their pelts. The pelts are sold for expensive fashion coats, under the name 'Swakara', through the Hudson's Bay auctions in London. A small amount of commercial cereal production takes place in the Grootfontein area, but production of maize and wheat is far below Namibia's domestic requirements. Despite the decline of peasant agriculture, this sector was still supplying an estimated 40 per cent of Namibia's grain needs in 1987.[16]

In the early 1980s farming collapsed, mainly as a result of drought and market changes. The cattle herd was reduced by a third, and karakul sheep numbers by three-quarters. The drought had an even more devastating effect on peasant farming and agriculture in the bantustans.[17]

An estimated 40,000 black Namibians are employed or live on white-owned farms. They are exposed to arbitrary and brutal treatment and paid low wages – often in the form of goods or food in kind.[18]

Other sectors

Domestic service for white households is a major source of employment for black Namibians, especially for women and youths or children. Like farm workers, domestic workers are unprotected by legislation and at the mercy of their employers.[19]

Manufacturing industry consists mostly of small processing plants, workshops and repair facilities, and accounts for only 5 per cent of GDP. Such industry is overwhelmingly based in Windhoek.[20]

The service and transport sectors have been two of the few growth areas since the late 1970s recession, but the most significant increase has been in administrative, military and

Meat processing

bureaucratic employment.

The imposition of bantustan administrations and the subsequent establishment of second-tier authorities with their various departments necessitated a substantial increase in employment and expenditure in this sector. In addition, some 20,000 Namibians have been recruited or conscripted into the occupation forces, though it is not likely that more than half of these are in full-time military employment. In real terms, the contribution to the GDP of the 'general government' sector nearly doubled between 1976 and 1984: in contrast agriculture and fishing declined by more than 50 per cent and construction by 37 per cent.[21]

The establishment of bantustan and related administrations has resulted in the growth of a small but significant black bureaucratic elite. In 1985 more than 37,000 Namibians were employed by the various administrations in the territory. To a much lesser extent this process has been accompanied by the development of a tiny black managerial and entrepeneurial class. The vast majority of black Namibians have not benefited by these changes, and their economic situation has deteriorated with the recession.[22]

Women pounding millet

BANTUSTANS AND MIGRANT LABOUR

Almost without exception, the mines, industries and commercial agricultural enterprises are situated in the areas of Namibia set aside under the 1964 Odendaal plan for white occupation (*see Chapter 2*). There are few formal employment opportunities in the bantustans outside the military and administrative structures and, in the north, the network of small trading stores and bars known as 'cuca shops'.

The bantustans are reservoirs of labour and depositories for the unemployed, sick and aged, especially for women and children not required as labour in the white-owned sector of the economy. This is made clear by population distribution statistics which show women substantially outnumbering men in the bantustans, and a higher proportion of children than elsewhere. In almost all the bantustans more than half the population is under 18. Even according to official figures, fewer than a quarter of people living in the bantustans are economically active.[23]

In Ovambo, the most populous area of Namibia, estimates derived from the 1970 census showed almost twice as many women as men in the 15-59 age group, while official figures in 1980/1 showed the female population exceeding the male population by some 70,000. Women bear much of the burden of agricultural production and childcare in the bantustans.[24]

The restriction of African residence largely to the impoverished bantustans has ensured a continued supply of migrant labour. Statistics are no longer kept, but it is generally estimated that at least half of all African

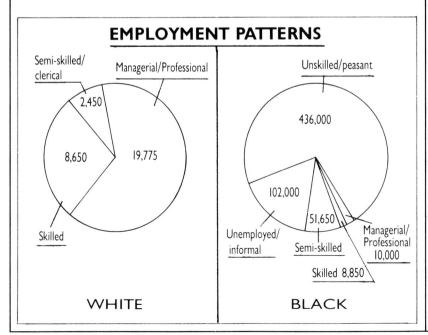

EMPLOYMENT PATTERNS

WHITE

- Semi-skilled/clerical: 2,450
- Managerial/Professional: 19,775
- Skilled: 8,650

BLACK

- Unskilled/peasant: 436,000
- Unemployed/informal: 102,000
- Semi-skilled: 51,650
- Skilled: 8,850
- Managerial/Professional: 10,000

workers in employment are migrant labourers.[25]

The migrant labour system has given the administration and employers greater power to set lower wages for all black workers and to control the allocation of labour to different sectors and enterprises. The temporary nature of employment has also made it difficult for workers to organise into trade unions and other structures.

The restriction of unwanted workers and their dependants to the bantustans has the political objective of removing Africans from areas occupied by whites. It provides a rationalisation for paying wages at the lowest possible rate for a single adult, ignoring his or her dependants and failing to provide medical and other social services for workers' families, as it is argued that families can support themselves through subsistence agriculture. In fact, surveys of migrant workers show that almost without exception they are driven to take up work out of economic necessity.[26]

CONTROL OF LABOUR

Until 1972 recruitment and control of migrant labour was conducted by the SWA Native Labour Association (SWANLA),

Men are 'handcuffed' by slips of paper. They must have permits to seek work, permits to be in the area for any purpose other than to seek work, service contracts to prove that they are working, passes to prove that they are schoolboys and too young to carry passes, certificates of registration authorising residence in the area, permits to travel, tax receipts, exemptions from night curfew. Passes and permits constitute their licence to live; they may move nowhere without joining the interminable queue at the government office for stamps of authority on their passes. No African in the Police Zone may buy a railway ticket without a pass issued by his employer or an authorised official. No African in a Reserve may leave it except by permit or in order to work for a White employer. Men have been reduced to mere labour units.

South African writer Ruth First describing the pass laws in 1963

which allocated workers to employers regardless of their skills or preferences. Workers signed contracts of 6 to 24 months – breaking the contract was a criminal offence. Workers were forced by the pass laws to return to the bantustans after the expiry of their contracts – no African was allowed to spend more than 72 hours in a 'white' area without official approval.

Changes were made to the system after the nationwide strike of 1971-2 (*see 'Labour Relations' below*). SWANLA was abolished and replaced with a network of labour bureaux operated mainly by bantustan authorities, but the essentials of the system remained in place.

The migrant labour regime was more substantially modified in 1977 when, as part of the South African effort to steer the territory towards carefully controlled 'independence', the pass laws were abolished. More limited restrictions on the mobility of labour remained, in that workers were required to register contracts through the labour bureaux. However, the large mining companies soon began to bypass the bureaux in order to recruit labour directly from the bantustans.[27]

The removal of legislative restrictions on the mobility of labour established a partially open labour market, but the social and economic consequences were not catered for. Huge peri-urban squatter areas have grown up as thousands of African families deserted impoverished rural areas or escaped from conditions of near-slavery on white-owned farms. Unemployment and homelessness in urban

Workers' barracks at Walvis Bay

> Most farm labourers round here live little better than slaves. They earn about R20 a month plus a fixed food ration, regardless of family size. Work as labourers on the surrounding farms is all that's available. People can hardly survive on the low pay, and, as a result, many of the children we look after at the hostel come to us with malnutrition. The white farmers round here are very hard; most of them do not allow their labourers the 'privilege' of growing a little food on their land.
>
> *Churchworker (quoted in Smith 1986, p. 39)*

Farmworker transported on back of employer's van

and surrounding areas has escalated rapidly and there are indications that there are large remittances of food from hard-pressed rural households to feed relatives in the towns. Only a small number of people have benefited from the changes.[28]

The migrant-labour system continues, kept in motion mainly by economic rather than legislative controls. Low wages mean that few African workers can afford to bring their families to the urban areas, while the lack of suitable accommodation makes such moves even more difficult. Employers continue to hire African workers on short-term contracts without any guarantees of renewal, and to house them in large all-male dormitories known as compounds or hostels. These are usually isolated from local communities and in many cases are controlled by armed guards.[29]

UNEMPLOYMENT

There are only incomplete official statistics for unemployment in Namibia, and the situation is complicated by the large numbers of people engaged in peasant agriculture and informal economic activities. It is clear, however, that unemployment is very high, even by the standards of developing countries, and that it has grown rapidly over the past decade. Almost all the unemployed are black.

The official figures show that unemployment grew from 12.3 per cent in 1975 to 20.6 per cent in 1984.[30] In a 1986 survey of Katutura residents, 43 per cent of workers stated that they were unemployed.[31] Surveys of 13 urban areas carried out by the National Building and Investment Corporation between 1984 and 1986 showed that more than a third of the economically active population was unemployed – rates were worst in small towns and squatter settlements. The survey stated that the situation was even worse in the bantustans, although no statistics were available.[32]

There are no state unemployment benefits for African workers. To survive, many unemployed people engage in informal economic activities – odd jobs or repair work, street selling and so on. Such activities account for between 10 and 20 per cent of urban employment, but the authorities harass and attempt to suppress the informal sector.[33]

WAGES AND LABOUR CONDITIONS

Wages reflect the divisions imposed on Namibian society, with white men earning the highest salaries and African women the lowest. Domestic and farm workers are the most poorly paid, while workers in mining and manufacturing are generally

paid more, although wages are still low and they often have more dependants and higher overheads.

> I am the only breadwinner in my whole family and I support my five children, my parents and my husband. As a result, we all live in poverty . . .
>
> I am not allowed to have my own children with me in Windhoek while I look after my employer's child. I miss my children all the time, and long to see them. But the fare home costs R20 so if I go to see my children, I have even less money to send home for food.
>
> *Domestic worker (quoted in Smith 1986, p. 32)*

In 1986 it was calculated that the minimum monthly household income needed to keep a family of six alive in Windhoek was R394 (*see Chapter 4*). In comparison, the wages of domestic workers were between R50 and R70 a month while wages of workers in the food industry were estimated at between R150 and R180. The starting wage of a worker in the Windhoek municipality was R174 in 1986, but according to one report workers received only R58 after deductions for accommodation. In Katutura, a third of workers were earning under R100 a month in 1986 and two-thirds under R200.[34]

Wages are determined by individual employers – there is no national minimum wage and rates vary extensively between and within the different sectors of the economy. No industry-wide bargaining structures exist. The official policy of the South African-installed administration in Windhoek is that 'wage determination should be a function of the market forces'.[35]

In many sectors real wages have declined as a result of inflation, and workers have achieved wage adjustments only after strikes or protest actions. However, salaries of public servants, including teachers and nurses, rose substantially in the late 1970s as the South African regime attempted to build support for the DTA administration.[36]

There are few legislative restraints on the exploitation of labour. The Conditions of Employment Act, which was introduced in 1986, lays down weak standards for maximum working hours and annual leave and specifies that workers have to be given formal contracts of employment. However, the Act does not apply to domestic or farm workers and there is little evidence that it has been enforced in other sectors. Labour matters are overseen by a National Labour Council which consists of representatives of the authorities, employers and the mainly white- dominated staff associations.[37]

Pensions and disability allowances discriminate against black workers (see Chapter 4) and black workers are not legally entitled to any compensation for dismissal, or to unemployment benefit.[38]

Working conditions are often dirty, dangerous and unhealthy. Legislation provides workers with little protection and they are exposed to racism, abuse and beatings in work-places. On farms, where historically white farmers have been empowered to flog workers, there have been numerous cases in which work-

ers have been brutally assaulted or killed by employers for minor misdemeanours.[39]

Details of conditions in the mines were disclosed by the general secretary of the Mineworkers Union of Namibia, Ben Ulenga, in 1987. He reported that miners received a poor diet consisting mainly of bread and maize meal and were given no food when they were underground. Black miners were usually housed in prison-like male-only compounds surrounded by barbed-wire fencing and patrolled by security guards.[40]

Housing conditions at the Rossing uranium mine are better than at the other mines, in part owing to the high level of international publicity given to the mine, but the UN Council for Namibia has expressed concern over the health of black workers

who work with radioactive material and are housed near the radioactive-tailings dumps. Workers at other mines have been exposed to health risks through arsenic and lead poisoning.[41]

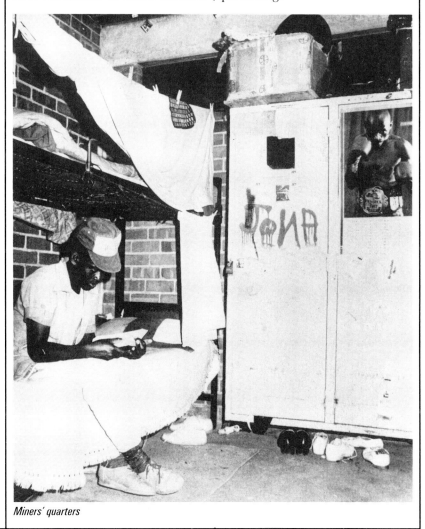

Miners' quarters

LABOUR RELATIONS

The suppression of worker organisation has been essential to the exploitation of labour in Namibia. Trade unions face harassment and repression and worker protests have been violently suppressed by the police and army. Labour relations are regulated by the Wage and Industrial Conciliation Ordinance of 1952, which sets out detailed negotiating procedures and imposes restrictions on unions. The ordinance originally excluded Africans from its provisions.[42]

An amendment to the legislation in 1978 allowed for the registration of unions representing African workers, but further restrictions were imposed on unions seeking registration. They were prohibited from affiliating to political parties or having any financial arrangements with political parties, and their finances and constitutions had to be approved by the industrial registrar.

Once registered, unions have to follow detailed and often lengthy procedures for wage negotiations and are prohibited from taking strike action while agreements are in force. Strikes in 'essential services' are illegal.[43]

In 1987 a commission headed by a South African expert, Professor Wiehahn, was appointed by the MPC administration to draw up proposals for a new industrial-relations system. Its chairman was reported to be against collective bargaining and to be considering in-house liaison committees.[44]

The history of worker organisation in Namibia goes back at least to the first recorded strike at the Gross Otavi mine in 1893. Workers have always made both economic and political demands, and the history of the trade-union movement is closely tied to that of the liberation struggle. SWAPO itself was founded by contract workers in the late 1950s.

Growing resistance to the contract-labour system, and increasing political awareness, led to a general strike of contract workers in December 1971, which was initiated by the SWAPO Youth League. By the second month of the strike, some 20,000 workers had taken action, affecting 23 urban centres as well as some rural areas where farm workers joined the protest.

In the face of ruthless police harassment, the strikers returned to their families in the northern bantustans, where they continued to organise. Their activities merged with peasant resistance, and a generalised uprising began in the Ovambo bantustan as people attacked police patrols and bantustan officials.

To crush resistance, the South African authorities sealed off the bantustan, imposed a state of emergency and dispatched troops and police who detained, tortured and killed people. As a result, hundreds more Namibians joined SWAPO's guerrilla army, leading to a rapid escalation of the liberation war.[45]

Intense repression and concessions by the authorities ended the strike. In subsequent years, worker militancy manifested itself in several strikes and protest actions and in the evasion of the pass laws. There were at least 70 strikes between June 1973 and June 1975 alone, and large strikes occurred in the mines and at fish-canning and meat-processing plants in the late 1970s and early 1980s.[46]

Much of the organisation of workers was carried out by the SWAPO-aligned National Union of Namibian Workers (NUNW). The union's organisers have

Striking miners voice their demands

May Day protest, 1988

been harassed and repeatedly detained without trial, and in 1980 the union's offices were shut down and its assets seized by the authorities. The NUNW was forced underground.[47]

In a further effort to counter the NUNW, the authorities have promoted in-house liaison committees or compliant trade unions, the most prominent of which has been the Namibia Trade Union (NTU). However, these unions have gained little support from black workers. The South West African Confederation of Labour (SWACOL), a federation consisting mostly of staff associations representing white civil servants and public-sector employees, has proved equally unattractive to black workers.[48]

With few facilities to organise the widely dispersed workforce, independent-union organisers in Namibia face great difficulties and constant harassment by the authorities. Nevertheless, as a result of NUNW

activities, five major industrial unions were formed between late 1986 and mid-1988.

Some 6,000 workers were represented by the Namibian Food and Allied Workers Union (NAFAU), and over 12,000 by the Mineworkers Union of Namibia (MUN), which established a presence at all the major mines. The Metal and Allied Namibian Workers Union (MANWU), with about 8,000 members in 1987, was established to organise workers in the metal industry and related sectors. The unions were involved in a number of disputes, and there were several strikes and protest actions at mines and in the fishing and meat- processing sectors during 1986 and 1987. Early in 1988 the Namibian Public Workers Union (NAPWU) was launched and in July the Namibian Transport and Allied Workers Union (NATAU) became the fifth industrial union in the NUNW fold.[49]

All the NUNW-affiliated

unions have campaigned on wider political issues as well as representing workers' economic interests. This was dramatically underscored in June 1988, when tens of thousands of workers held a two-day general strike or 'stay-away' in support of students who were boycotting classes in protest at army bases near schools. The workers demanded the removal of SADF bases from the vicinity of schools, the release of all detainees and the immediate withdrawal of police and military units from townships. The strike, which was co-ordinated by the NUNW unions through their shop-steward committees, was the largest and most significant worker action since the 1971 contract workers' strike.[50]

A response to the repression and exploitation of the Namibian people, the political activities of the unions have reflected the vital role that workers have played in the national liberation struggle.

Ben Ulenga, miners' leader, addressing workers

Mineworkers Union of Namibia, CDM branch

1968 One thousand Walvis Bay fish-cannery workers strike over pay

April 1971 Strike by fish-cannery workers at Walvis Bay and Luderitz

December 1971 to January 1972 Up to 20,000 workers in general strike against contract-labour system. Mines, transport system and municipalities crippled

February 1972 Walvis Bay fish-cannery workers strike over working conditions and contract labour; municipal workers at Otjiwarongo strike for higher wages

January 1975 Strikes over wages at a number of firms in Keetmanshoop

July 1975 Miners at Otjihase refuse to go on shift in protest at conditions

March 1978 Two thousand Katutura hostel residents stage two-day strike after violent clashes and police killings in Windhoek

December 1978 Week-long strike by 2,000 workers at Rossing uranium mine, over pay and health conditions

January 1979 Two hundred striking workers sacked at Kranzberg mine, Omaruru; 500 workers strike at Uis tin mine; police raid Tsumeb hostel after strike threatened

April 1979 Almost the entire 5,000-strong black work-force at CDM diamond mine stage protest strike over food

February 1981 Luderitz lobster fishermen strike over wages

November 1981 One hundred workers sacked during strike at Damara Meat Packers factory in Windhoek

October 1982 Five thousand CDM workers down tools in protest at dismissal of two workers

January 1983 Women workers at Table Top fish processing plant in Walvis Bay strike over wages

April 1983 Entire black work-force at TCL's Otjihase mine strike over working conditions – over 100 sacked

November 1983 Katutura taxi drivers hold one day strike in protest at 'victimisation' by authorities

September 1986 Workers at Swavleis meat-processing plant in Windhoek down tools over wage cuts

October 1986 Workers at Swavleis' Okahandja abattoir strike; strike at Taurus Chemical plant in Luderitz in protest at dismissal of 16 workers; 3,000 CDM workers boycott official celebrations to mark 50th anniversary of company

January 1987 Two-week strike by 500 Luderitz lobster fishermen

March 1987 Five hundred miners at Klein Aub dismissed after striking over retrenchment conditions

May 1987 Six hundred Swavleis workers in Windhoek fired after strike over wages – reinstated after consumer boycotts threatened

June 1987 Taurus Chemical workers strike over dismissal of worker

July-August 1987 Four thousand workers at three TCL mines strike over wages and conditions and demand management support for Namibian independence – dismissed and selectively re-employed

December 1987 CDM work-force in 14-hour strike after management confiscates money from employee

National Union of Namibian Workers meeting

SWAPO flags at union rally

4 LIVING CONDITIONS

The South African regime has stamped its apartheid policies on all aspects of life in Namibia. Economic exploitation has been accompanied by segregation and inequality in health care and housing. The result has been overcrowded, unhealthy and impoverished living conditions for the vast majority of black Namibians.

HOUSING

Residential segregation, underpinned by social and economic inequalities, remains the dominant feature of housing in Namibia, despite the removal of legislative restrictions (*see Chapter 2*). Whites live mainly in flats near the centres of towns, in detached houses in the suburbs, or on farms.

A small number of black Namibians, many of them employees of the central and second-tier administrations, have moved into the 'white' areas, or have built new houses on the outskirts of Katutura and other townships. The vast majority are forced through economic necessity to live in bleak box-like accommodation in segregated townships, in single-sex dormitory complexes, or in unserviced shack settlements.[1]

Accommodation in rural areas is at best rudimentary, especially for workers on commercial farms. Often farmers simply leave workers to erect shelters, without providing finance or materials.[2]

People living in the bantustans have little access to loans or financial assistance in erecting housing. Many homes in the war zones have been destroyed by South African troops. In Ovambo a kilometre-wide strip along the border with Angola was forcibly cleared of population to create a military free-fire zone – villages were destroyed and tens of

White residence

Black township housing

thousands of people uprooted. Forced removals for military purposes have also taken place in the Kavango bantustan. Those affected by removals have not been compensated.[3]

In other parts of the country Namibians have been forcibly moved and their houses destroyed as the authorities have imposed residential segregation. Tens of thousands of farm workers and tenants have also been evicted from farms during drives

to commercialise and mechanise agriculture.

Most township houses lack hot water or flush toilets and many are without electricity. Roads are usually untarred and street lighting is seldom provided. Refuse collection and sewerage facilities are inadequate, leading to unhealthy living conditions. Insufficient and expensive transport results in township residents walking long distances to their work places.[4]

Houses in the officially proclaimed townships are usually rented out by municipal and other local authorities, but new housing is in most cases only for sale. Building programmes lag far behind demand. The authorities have deliberately attempted to slow down urban migration by not providing sufficient housing.

In 1987 the National Building and Investment Corporation, which is responsible for house-construction programmes in local-authority areas, stated that it needed to construct nearly 23,000 low-income housing units to meet existing demand. The backlog was expected to increase to over 53,000 by 1995. The vast majority of Africans in need of housing could not afford to purchase even the cheapest units. Many families who had obtained houses were unable to maintain repayments or pay rent and were threatened with eviction.[5]

Chronic overcrowding results from the housing shortage. A survey of Khomasdal in 1982 showed an average of 13 people occupying every rented two-bedroomed house; in some houses there were up to 35 people. In Katutura in 1986 average occupancy per house was nearly 8, rising to 11 in the poorest sector. Many people are forced to live in old cars, or shacks erected in back yards.[6]

Overcrowding is reflected in population-density statistics: 14 people per hectare in Windhoek, 40 in Khomasdal and 85 in Katutura.[7]

Tens of thousands of people live in shack settlements near towns, or dispersed on farms. Large settlements, in some cases with populations greater than those of nearby towns, have been established near Oshakati, Ondangua, Okahandja and Rehoboth. There is little public transport, water usually has to be drawn from dams or nearby taps and there are no sewerage facilities. Disease and sickness is widespread.[8]

As has been described in

Family's accomodation, Tsumkwe, Bushmanland bantustan

Katutura single quarters

Chapter 3, thousands of male workers, most of them migrants, are accommodated in bleak single-sex compounds, often packed ten or more to a room. These compounds are sealed off or patrolled by armed police, and police raids on residents have led to violent confrontations. Even where housing outside compounds is available to migrant workers, they are usually unable to obtain housing loans.[9]

HEALTH AND WELFARE

Colonial and apartheid policies have resulted in low life expectancy, high infant mortality and a high incidence of the diseases associated with poverty amongst black Namibians. On the other hand, whites in Namibia enjoy standards of health care comparable to those of advanced industrialised countries.

National infant mortality rates are not available, but it has been estimated that black children are

Black children are seven times more likely to die in infancy than white children

Cemetery in Katutura

seven times more likely to die in infancy than white children. In Windhoek in 1981, infant mortality rates for blacks were 178 per thousand and for whites 28 per thousand. Life expectancy for whites is between 68 and 72 years, for blacks between 42 and 52 years.[10]

A study by the British-based charity Oxfam in 1986 noted: 'In Oxfam's experience some of the worst examples of chronic poverty and suffering in Africa are to be found amongst Namibia's black population, alongside the wealthy and privileged lifestyle enjoyed by the minority white population.'[11]

Most of the diseases which affect black Namibians derive from material poverty and poor diet. A survey of urban areas carried out between 1984 and 1986 by the semi-official National Building and Investment Corporation concluded: 'Average household incomes are generally insufficient to ensure basic subsistence. The average household, therefore, lives way below the breadline.'[12]

A survey of pre-school black children carried out in three communities in 1986 showed that a quarter of the children were malnourished while 11 per cent suffered from acute malnutrition. The survey did not include the war zones, where conditions are even worse.[13]

Tuberculosis, gastro-enteritis and measles, which have been all but eliminated as a threat to white children, are major killers of black infants. Malaria and bilharzia are prevalent in the north and outbreaks of bubonic plague have occurred.[14]

High rates of alcoholism and mental illness amongst black Namibians result from the pressures of poor housing, poverty and migrant labour. Facilities for treating mentally ill black Namibians are restricted to a small number of beds set aside in the general wards of two state hospitals.[15]

Health services

The health services established under the South African occupation emphasise curative rather than preventive measures, and high-technology services suited to the affluent white population which can afford private medicine.

The services were established on a segregated basis and the best facilities put at the sole disposal of whites. The Administration for Whites controls many of the major hospitals and resources. Institutions run by the other authorities are supposedly open to all, but economic inequalities and residential separation result in continuing segregation.[16]

Health services for black Namibians have deteriorated in many areas since 1980, when they were taken over from the central administration by the second-tier authorities. Inequalities were exacerbated as impoverished black authorities attempted to run health departments with little finance. Five of the black health authorities were subsequently run on an agency basis by the Administration for Whites.

New whites-only facilities were established in the early 1980s, and a hospital in the seaside town of Swakopmund was built with separate wings for black and white patients.[17]

It has been estimated that on average ten times more is spent on the health of each white person than on each black Namibian. In 1983 per capita expenditure on health by the white authority was R233; expenditure by black authorities ranged from R4 to R56. Ninety-five per cent of doctors were white.[18]

Hospitals serving whites, which have the most modern medical technology, are under-utilised – for example a hospital built in 1982 in Keetmanshoop with 200 beds never had more than 23 patients at any time during its first year of operation. Hospitals for blacks are overcrowded and short of staff, drugs and equipment. Facilities in urban areas, such as Katutura hospital, are inadequate, but the situation is far worse in rural areas.[19]

Health in the north

Only 30 of Namibia's 293 medical practitioners were based in the Ovambo bantustan in 1987, although over half the population lives there. In the other northern bantustans there were a further 17 doctors.[20]

Many clinics and small hospitals in the northern bantustans were established and run by European missionary societies. These facilities have been systematically starved of funds and supplies by the authorities. Some have been burnt down or sabotaged by South African troops. Staff suspected of aiding or treating SWAPO combatants have been detained without trial and tortured. Church doctors and staff have been driven out of Namibia through the refusal of

Clinic in northern Namibia

Many people come to the hospital who have been beaten up or suffered mutilation at the hands of the South African army . . .

People come to us with arms and legs broken as well as cuts and bruises and other wounds. One man had both his ears cut off. Others have black eyes and bruised faces. Most of these victims manage to get to the hospital one way or another. Sometimes they are brought on home-made stretchers.

Before the war made it impossible, our hospital operated seven mobile clinics. These gave services like antenatal care to women living far away. Staff were sent to attend on expectant mothers. This is no longer possible. Last week one women gave birth to her baby alone at home. The baby died, but she had to stay there for three days. She could not get to the hospital. She arrived here on foot, and died soon after . . .

The hospital has been without electricity for many months. We cannot use fridges to store our medicines. The generator was old and broke down. There is no light. Even the paraffin lamps are not working well, so we use candles. Sometimes we do not get any medical supplies because they think we use these for the fighters.

Nurse at hospital in the war zone quoted in Allison, 1986, pp. 45-6

work permits and visas.[21]

People living in the bantustans often have to travel long distances to clinics and hospitals – the dusk-to-dawn curfew in Ovambo together with other security legislation has made travel much more difficult. Civilians have been shot on sight at

night, and in several cases people seeking urgent medical attention after the curfew have been killed. Health workers based in the war zones have been killed, detained and tortured, and preventive health work has declined as a result.[22]

Remaining health facilities in the north have been progressively militarised, as the South African army has tried to 'win hearts and minds' through control of health and other services. By 1985 the majority of doctors in the north were army personnel working under military command. The health services in Ovambo had effectively been taken over by the army, and a colonel was appointed director of the bantustan medical services.[23]

As a result of friction between the military and bantustan authorities, army medical personnel were suddenly withdrawn from Ovambo in 1986. Local people were informed through leaflets that treatment would have to be obtained at military bases. Army personnel continued to be deployed in the health services of the other northern bantustans.[24]

At refugee centres in Angola and Zambia SWAPO has established a comprehensive health programme. Through practical experience in dealing with the health needs of tens of thousands of refugees, it has established the framework for a new Namibian health service to be implemented after independence. The liberation movement emphasises preventive community-oriented health, basic nutrition and health education.[25]

Pensions and childcare

Most retired or elderly black Namibians barely survive on state pensions. In 1986 pensions for Africans ranged between R55 and R70 monthly, depending on the second-tier authority making the payment. Pensions for whites were R150 monthly. Many whites supplement state pensions with more substantial payments from private schemes, for which few blacks are eligible. Pensions for blacks are paid irregularly in many areas, and pensioners often have to travel long distances and wait for hours to receive their payments.[26]

Institutions for the aged are run by private organisations, and those for blacks rely on charity. In 1986 the only institution for elderly black people in Katutura, which catered for about fifty people, was without electricity and had only one tap.[27]

Black workers seldom qualify for or can afford to join company pension funds or the medical aid schemes to which white workers subscribe. Many black workers have not received occupational disablement payments for injuries at work. As compensation is calculated as a percentage of wages earned payments to black workers are lower.[28]

Facilities for the care of elderly or disabled black Namibians are rudimentary. There are virtually no state facilities for childcare, but churches and community organisations run

We have become old. We are starving. Often we do not have anything to eat at all. What we get is a pension which we use to buy things, but everything is so expensive all I can afford is a mealie meal. This does not give us enough nutrition, but we cannot afford to buy anything else. Often the pension is so irregular, we wonder when the next payment will be made. We do not know the rules of those people who distribute the money. We do not know why it comes so irregularly.

Pensioner (quoted in Allison, 1986, p. 13)

some institutions. The burden of care for children and old people falls heavily on impoverished families, especially in the bantustans where men are often away working as migrant labourers and women have to rear children as well as work the land.

No state maternity benefits are available. An extensive campaign is waged to control black population growth through Depo-provera contraceptive injections and sterilisation. Depo-provera, the use of which is banned in the USA where it is manufactured, is often given to women without their consent. Mobile vans tour farms and factories injecting women, usually at the request of white bosses. There have been numerous cases where sterilisation of black women has been carried out without their knowledge or consent during surgery or caesarian births.[29]

5 EDUCATION, INFORMATION AND IDEAS

Black Namibians have always been denied the educational, cultural and sporting facilities available to the colonisers of their country. The South African administration has kept a tight grip on the media and other means of communication, while Namibian culture has been suppressed or distorted to promote apartheid.

As Namibians have struggled to gain their freedom and assert their national identity and culture, conflicts with the occupation authorities have erupted in the areas of education, the media and culture.

EDUCATION

Both German and South African colonial policy allowed for only limited, missionary education, which rigorously suppressed Namibian culture but provided some primary literacy. During the 1950s and 1960s, the ideology of 'Bantu Education' held sway. In the words of South African Prime Minister Verwoerd, this system was aimed at ensuring that 'there is no place for the native in the European community, above the level of certain forms of labour'.[1]

Bantu Education aimed to expand primary education to increase the number of literate workers and, by deliberately suppressing secondary and tertiary education, to prevent black economic and social advance. There was no secondary education available in Namibia until 1953, and secondary schooling was only provided in the northern bantustans in 1961.

Education was strictly segregated according to population group. Mother-tongue instruc-

tion was maintained for the first four years to establish 'ethnic identity' and separate syllabuses stressing apartheid concepts were drawn up. Mission schools were brought under state control and segregated education departments established. Education was made free and compulsory only for white children, who were provided with the finest schools and facilities.[2]

Control of education

Black education has been modified to accommodate economic

and political changes over the past twenty years, but the legacy of Bantu Education remains. Education in Namibia is still segregated, grossly unequal and ideologically moulded by apartheid.

The Department of National Education, which is controlled by the South African-appointed authorities in Windhoek, is responsible for higher and technical education and some black schools. Most schools are controlled by second-tier authorities.

EDUCATION EXPENDITURE – 1985 Rands per pupil		
Education Authority	No of Pupils	Expend per pupil
White	16,403	1,760*
Tswana	737	1,496
Coloured	15,391	883
Baster	10,655	784
Damara	8,889	758
Nama	14,130	681
'National'	35,721	548
Herero	14,474	504
Caprivi	16,827	446
Kavango	29,791	444
Ovambo	172,584	280

* Estimate

Source: WUS 1987

This has perpetuated radical inequalities. In 1986/7, nearly four times more was allocated to each white child than to each child in schools controlled by the Ovambo bantustan administration.[3] A relatively small number of schools are run by the churches, although most have been closed or taken over by various administrations. Many of these schools serve out-lying areas, particularly in the war zones, or provide boarding facilities. Some of them, such as the African Methodist Episcopal School at Gibeon, draw pupils from all over Namibia and actively promote concepts of national unity and independence.

The church schools suffer from restrictive state subsidies and political pressure by the authorities. Pupils, teachers and principals are harassed and some schools have been attacked by troops.[4]

Inequality in schools

Overcrowding, unqualified teachers, shortages of books and equipment and a lack of class-room space are the norm in black schools. Classes of 80 to 100 pupils are not unusual. Many primary schools can only accommodate pupils by running two separate daily sessions – morning and afternoon. Some 40,000 children are obliged to attend the afternoon sessions. Libraries, laboratories, sports facilities, principals' offices are lacking at many black schools.

The Department of National Education disclosed in 1987 that there was a shortage of 3,000 classrooms, while another study calculated that the number of available classrooms needed to be doubled in the following fifteen years to meet demand and eliminate the backlog. In white schools, there is one classroom for every 10 pupils, but in Ovambo bantustan schools there is one for every 59 pupils.[5]

In white schools, there is one teacher for every 13 pupils; in Ovambo there is one for every 44

EDUCATION EXPENDITURE PER PUPIL 1985
Six largest education departments (Rands)

Department	Rands
White	1,760
Coloured	883
'National'	548
Caprivi	446
Kavango	444
Ovambo	280

Source: WUS 1987

Church-run school, Gibeon, Namaland bantustan

pupils. Eight out of ten teachers in the mid-1980s were unqualified. A study carried out in 1980 showed that the vast majority of teachers in black schools had no more than one year of secondary education. In some schools, the qualifications of the teachers are the same as those of the pupils they instruct or lower.[6]

The proportion of unqualified teachers increases every year, as less than half the demand for new trained teachers is met. While there is a shortage of training facilities for black teachers, in 1985 the new Wind-hoek College of Education, reserved for whites, was operating at less than a fifth of its capacity.[7]

In the bantustans, teacher shortages have been used as a justification for stationing white South African troops at schools. However, there has been con-siderable popular resistance to the soldier-teachers who in many cases have been armed and unqualified to teach. They were withdrawn from Ovambo in 1985 after allegations that they had undermined the bantustan education authority and sabo-taged one of the schools in an effort to discredit PLAN, the SWAPO combat force.[8]

The lack of funds, classrooms and qualified teachers in black schools, together with wider social and economic discrimina-tion and the fact that education for black children is not compulsory, results in one of the highest failure and drop-out rates in Africa. In 1984, one out of three pupils did not finish the first year of schooling while 70 per cent of those who reached the final year of primary school received no secondary education. Only a fifth of pupils overall were in secondary school, and less than 1 per cent completed the final year of schooling.[9]

The result of the high drop-out rate is that while the majority of Namibians have received some schooling, most cannot read or write. Estimates of illiteracy range between 50 and 70 per cent.[10]

Afrikaans has been the main teaching language at secondary level. However, as a result of campaigning by students and parents, it has been dropped in most schools in favour of English-medium instruction.[11]

Schools are forced to teach the South African curriculum used in the Cape Province but some local variations based on earlier Bantu Education syllabuses persist. These distort Namibia's past and attempt to inculcate apartheid stereotypes. Some schools controlled by the churches, as well as a few independent community schools, teach the syllabus used in the independent Southern African states of Lesotho, Botswana and Swaziland. There have also been moves to introduce syllabuses and textbooks used in schools established outside Namibia by SWAPO, but some books have been banned by the authorities.

Higher education

Higher educational and vocational training facilities for black Namibians are limited. In 1986 only 104 black students were undergoing full-time technical training at tertiary level.

An institute for higher education in Windhoek, known simply as the Academy and referred to by the authorities as

'Namibia's university', provides the only university-level education in Namibia, but most of the 3,000 students at the institution study at pre-university level – only 12 degrees were issued in 1987. Students have protested at a lack of academic freedom and restrictions on student organisation at the Academy. Many Namibian students, including most white university students, study at South African universities.[12]

> We find in our schools glaring irregularities to do with syllabuses, curricula, teacher qualifications, school fees, recreational facilities and many more...
>
> Our culture is despised and our students are taught the cultural norms and values of the colonialists at the expense of our own cultural values . . .
>
> It should be stressed that education is almost exclusively reserved for white children in Namibia. They enjoy the privileges of compulsory and free education while our black pupils have to struggle to get to school, let alone universities, because they simply cannot afford it.
>
> *Hafeni Nghinamwaami, letter to* The Namibian *newspaper, 26.9.86*

Government adult-education and literacy programmes are very limited, but many programmes are run by the churches and community organisations. The Council of Churches, through its Non-Formal Education Unit, provides educational facilities to Namibians from all over the country. Many students leave the northern war zones to attend the unit in Windhoek, as military harassment and martial-law restrictions in the north make study difficult.[13]

Vocational training and adult-education facilities have also been established by large mining companies, Rossing especially, while CDM finances the elite secondary Concordia College. These educational projects largely began in the 1970s, when the companies were faced with a skilled labour shortage and came

under international and domestic pressure to end their illegal operations in Namibia.

Student and teacher struggles

Students have repeatedly rebelled against inferior and racist education over the past decades, and many young Namibians have gone into exile to study.

Student protests have taken place at secondary schools virtually every year since 1971. These have led to mass expulsions, the closure of schools, the dismissal of teachers and the detention or torture of pupils. Students have demanded the removal of racist teachers or soldiers, protested at discrimination, and demanded an end to military conscription which has been carried out through registration at schools since 1980. Boycotts and protests have also taken place at teacher-training colleges and other institutions.

In the war zones pupils have actively supported PLAN guerrillas. The army has responded to resistance in schools by closing them down, bombing and burning school buildings and detaining or killing students. In early 1987 at least 13 schools in the north, most of them run by churches, were attacked by South African troops and partially destroyed. Army bases have also been built near schools in an attempt to intimidate pupils and in the hope that the bases would thus be protected from guerrilla attacks.[14]

In 1984 students formed the Namibian National Students Organisation (NANSO), which has established branches in many secondary schools and training institutions as well as organised Namibian students at South African universities.

NANSO has campaigned for free compulsory education for all Namibians, an end to the prefect and cadet systems and the introduction of student representative councils. It has also campaigned against conscription and backed wider demands for Namibian independence.[15]

In 1988 a boycott of schools, which started in the north where pupils were demanding the removal of South African army bases from near schools, spread throughout the country. In June some 40,000 students led by NANSO and the SWAPO Youth League and supported by the NUNW unions, boycotted classes. Rallies and meetings were broken up by the police and army reinforcements were moved into urban areas.[16]

As students our involvement in the struggle must start with democratising our operational areas. The moment has come that we as students should start building democratic structures in our educational centres in order to be able to meet and act on the challenges of future society. We cannot speak of people's education without being organised at school level.

Paul Kalenga, NANSO President, 1987

Education in exile

To provide for the education of the tens of thousands of Namibians in exile, and to lay the basis for a new education system, SWAPO has set up a variety of educational projects. As well as pre-school facilities, primary and junior secondary schools have been established in Angola and Zambia, which are attended by about 7,000 to 8,000 Namibian children. Cuba also provides education for Namibian refugees. Syllabuses and textbooks have been prepared and teachers trained.

Extensive adult-literacy courses are run in refugee centres, the largest of which is at Kwanza Sul in Angola, where there are over 40,000 Namibian refugees.

Vocational training is provided by the SWAPO Secondary Technical School in Congo as well as the UN Vocational Training Centre at Sumbe in Angola. Higher education is conducted through the UN Institute for Namibia in Lusaka, which aims to train administrative and skilled personnel for an independent Namibia. By 1986 the institute had produced over 700 graduates. Some 4,000 Namibians are also studying through correspondence courses run by the Namibia Extension Unit in Lusaka, while Namibian students can be found studying on scholarships at institutions all over the world.[17]

NANSO meeting demands democratic representation

Worker stay-away in support of student boycott, June 1988: police patrol in Katutura

SWAPO-run school, Kwanza Sul refugee centre, Angola

MEDIA

Information, particularly about the liberation struggle and the war, is tightly controlled in Namibia. Radio, television and many publications are owned and editorially controlled by the South African authorities or collaborators. Newspapers, magazines and other publications are subject to South African censorship, while the gathering and dissemination of information is restricted by numerous apartheid laws.

Radio and television

The South West African Broadcasting Corporation (SWABC), which is controlled by the authorities through an appointed board, broadcasts political and cultural programmes in all the main Namibian languages. An analysis of political programmes in 1986 showed that nearly 30 per cent dealt with 'security' – almost entirely official military news releases – and 60 per cent with the South African-installed political and administrative structures. Only 10 per cent of programmes dealt with other political issues or events.[18]

Many Namibians tune in to SWAPO's Voice of Namibia, which broadcasts in the short- and medium-wave bands from other African countries. Voice of Namibia carries political comment, news, interviews with liberation-movement leaders and cultural or music programmes.[19]

Television was introduced to Namibia in 1981. Also controlled by the SWABC, it consists mainly of South African programmes broadcast in English and Afrikaans. TV reception is only available in certain parts of the country and the majority of viewers are in Windhoek.[20]

Press

Almost all Namibia's several daily and weekly newspapers are based in Windhoek and owned either by white businessmen or by political groups collaborating with the South African occupation. In the words of an editor of one of the dailies: 'The press in Namibia is primarily a Windhoek press and it ignores large parts of the country and of the community . . . it writes about the local political elite and is read by them.'[21]

Magazines produced by the churches, such as *Omukwetu* and *Omukuni*, circulate widely in the war zones, as does *The Namibian*, a weekly newspaper supporting Namibian independence under UN Resolution 435.

Publications which have exposed South African atrocities and torture and campaigned for Namibian independence have been repressed. Journalists have been assaulted by South African soldiers or police and foreign journalists expelled from the country. The offices of the *The Namibian* have been attacked on a number of occasions and its journalists harassed. The editor Gwen Lister was detained in mid-1988 for revealing police plans to impose a general State of Emergency to cope with nation-wide popular resistance. The *Omukwetu* printing press at Oniipa has been twice destroyed by South African agents and its editor was forced into exile in 1980.[22]

Various departments of the South African administration,

including the armed forces, produce propaganda magazines in various languages. Many of these are distributed free through schools and libraries.[23]

South African laws which restrict reporting include the Protection of Information Act, which was extended to Namibia prior to the inauguration of the MPC administration in 1985. The Police Act and Defence Act restrict reports on military and police matters. They are far-reaching – in 1975 the regime completely blanked out information on its invasion of Angola from Namibian bases, and reports on subsequent attacks have been tightly controlled.

Censorship is carried out by military and police authorities and through the South African Publications Control Board, which has banned the distribution or possession of many Namibian publications. SWAPO journals such as *Namibia Today* and the PLAN magazine *The Combatant*, which are distributed clandestinely in Namibia, are regularly listed in the *Government Gazette* as having been banned.

Censorship of daily and weekly newspapers is usually carried out less directly, as most Namibian newspapers belong to the South African Newspaper Press Union (NPU). The South African Media Council regulates the content of NPU-affiliated publications, which are thus exempt from the direct control of the Publications Control Board.

When the *Windhoek Observer* resigned from the NPU in 1984, eight issues of the newspaper were banned, and an outright ban on all further issues was imposed in August that year. This was lifted on appeal, but it resulted in the newspaper considerably toning down its criticism of the South African occupation.[24]

Control over the Press is also exercised through the Internal Security Act, in terms of which newspapers can be made to pay a deposit before publication. Both

the *Windhoek Observer* and *The Namibian* were forced to pay R20,000 deposits, but these were later set aside by the Supreme Court.[25]

At the end of 1987 SWAPO launched its own press agency, the Namibia Press Agency (NAMPA), to break through South African censorship and to raise the profile of Namibia internationally. With its headquarters in Luanda in Angola, and correspondents inside Namibia, NAMPA files reports on all aspects of the Namibian struggle, including military reports from its war correspondents. The Namibia Communications Centre in London, which was set up on the initiative of the Council of Churches in Namibia, also provides extensive information to the world media.[26]

RELIGION

The vast majority of Namibians are Christians. An estimated 80 per cent of the population belong to one or other of the Christian denominations, of which the Evangelical Lutheran Church in Namibia (ELCIN) and its partner the Evangelical Lutheran Church (ELC) are the largest. These churches grew out of the Finnish and Rhenish Missionary Societies respectively, but have been independent for decades. The Roman Catholic and Anglican churches also have a sizeable following. There are small minorities that belong to other religions, such as Islam.

All the main Christian denominations, with the exception of the white Dutch Reformed Church, are united in the Council of Churches (CCN), which was set up in 1978.

Church involvement in the struggle for freedom began in the 1940s and 1950s when the Namibian churches asserted their independence from European missions. Some individual church leaders such as Michael Scott played a prominent role in the international struggle for Namibian independence. A priest, Theophilus Hamutum-

bangela, was one of the founders of SWAPO.

A turning-point came in 1971 when the major churches combined in sending an open letter to the South African prime minister demanding Namibian independence. In the 1970s church leaders such as Anglican Bishops Colin Winter and Richard Wood helped to expose the brutal South African clampdown which followed the 1971-2 general strike. Both bishops were expelled from the territory by the authorities.[27]

Under the leadership of Bishops Dumeni (ELCIN), Fredrik (ELC), Kauluma (Anglican) and Haushiku (Roman Catholic), the Namibian churches have played an important role in the independence struggle during the 1980s. The CCN has helped with the establishment of trade union, student and community organisations. In the war zones the churches provide health, educational and social resources to local people, and they form an important part of community life throughout the territory. They also provide support for Namibian exiles, including a chaplaincy in the refugee camps.

Church procession, Katutura

We represent the conviction of over 75 per cent of the people in Namibia who suffer oppression, injury and death every day at the hands of the racist apartheid regime of the Republic of South Africa, which has ruled Namibia illegally for the last twenty years and continues to do so today.

The people of Namibia suffer in these ways because they struggle for the freedom and independence which are rightfully theirs.

In a special way the Church suffers persecution for its commitment to justice and peace . . .

Instead of independence and the ability to determine their own future, the Namibian people continue to suffer from a violation of their human rights such as restrictions on freedom of speech, assembly and movement within the country, travel abroad, visits by colleagues from other countries and the like.

We appeal to the Churches within Namibia and outside, and to governments, to renew their commitment to the liberation of Namibia, to speak and act on its behalf so that independence may be realized at an early date and an era of justice and peace may begin.

Statement by the Lutheran Roman Catholic and Anglican Bishops in Namibia, November 1986

Bishops Haushiku, Kauluma and Dumeni

Through international tours, open letters, public statements and pastoral addresses, the churches have sought to expose the suffering of Namibians under South African occupation, and have campaigned for the implementation of UN Resolution 435. They have sought international support through hosting church delegations from overseas. The bishops have taken legal action to secure the release of detainees held without trial and have attempted to have the courts revoke the curfew in the north.[28]

In May 1986 the major denominations, together with the Council of Churches, united with SWAPO and political and community groupings to launch a programme of action for independence called the Ai-Gams Declaration. The Ai-Gams signatories held large rallies and public protests (*see Chapter 8*).[29]

The participation of the churches in the independence struggle has exposed them to repression. Church leaders have been deported, prevented from travelling abroad, banned from speaking or being quoted, imprisoned, tortured and killed. Troops have invaded churches, rounded up congregations and sabotaged church schools, clinics and other facilities.[30]

CULTURE

The culture of Namibians has been systematically undermined by colonialism. Songs and dances were suppressed by missionaries, and culture has been neglected and distorted in colonial-education syllabuses. Apartheid ideology relegates African culture to a position of inferiority and, to promote division and segregation, emphasises and distorts differences between Namibians.

Government funds and resources have been channelled largely into facilities which serve the white minority. Theatres and cinemas cater mainly for whites and there are few cultural facilities in black areas. Culture, like education, falls under the authority of the second-tier administrations, and is thus dealt with in a segregated and unequal manner. The Administration for Whites, which has by far the largest culture budget, has promoted events such as art competitions which are exclusively reserved for whites.[31]

As part of its campaign to 'win hearts and minds', the South African Defence Force (SADF) has established cultural-front organisations such as Ezuva in the Kavango bantustan, Etango in Ovambo and Namwi in the Caprivi. These organisations promote bantustan concepts and are usually under the control of white officials. Through meetings, publications and lectures organised by the army, they urge people to support the South African armed forces and to act against SWAPO. Ezuva and Etango have also attempted to establish religious organisations in opposition to the main denominations and a student organisation has been set up in an attempt to counter NANSO.[32]

Cultural activity is an increasingly important aspect of the struggle for freedom. SWAPO believes that 'a living culture can never be divorced from the politics of the society of which it is a product'. The oneness of Namibia's people has become the unifying concept behind the optimistic cultural revival of the liberation struggle. Traditional songs and dances have been adapted, and dozens of 'freedom songs' composed to promote the independence struggle. Poetry, dance and music have also been transformed, while the SWAPO colours of blue, red and green are used by dressmakers and craft workers to popularise the liberation movement.[33]

Through SWAPO's Department of Culture Namibians in exile have established dance troupes, performance groups, choirs and musical ensembles, and written plays, poems and novels which use both traditional and modern cultural forms to promote national unity and project Namibian culture on to the world stage.

Cultural activities have also been carried out by student, church and community organisations in Namibia, as well as by the liberation movement itself. The growing importance of culture in the liberation strug-

John Muafangejo, internationally renowned Namibian artist who died in 1987

gle was reflected at a festival organised by NANSO in 1986. According to the organisers, the objective of the festival was to mobilise against the apartheid 'cultural onslaught', consolidate a 'resistance culture' and prepare the ground for a 'people's culture' to emerge.[34]

> The protracted struggle for national liberation in Namibia has set in motion a deep-going process of cultural renewal and assertion of a Namibian national identity. This cultural renewal, current in Namibia, is permeated with a profound sense of optimism.
>
> *From* Namibia: Culture and the Liberation Struggle, *SWAPO*

Onyeka, SWAPO cultural group

Children at church-run school in Gibeon enact drama of Kassinga massacre

SPORT

Although there are no legal restrictions against non-segregated sport, most sports are still segregated by team, club or league. The best sports facilities are used exclusively by whites, while those in black areas are often rudimentary. At school level, white school teams have refused to play against non-racial teams, while segregated institutions such as the College of Education field all-white teams. Police and Defence Force teams compete in many sports although black Namibian teams have refused to play with them. The occupation forces also organise competitions and provide sports training and equipment as part of the campaign to 'win hearts and minds'.[35]

Namibians, both black and white, are avid followers of sport, especially soccer, volleyball and netball, which are played at school level as well as between amateur club teams. Rugby is popular amongst whites and a variety of other sports are played.

As Namibia is not yet independent, there are no national teams which compete in the international sphere. 'South West African' teams are selected in some sports to play against South African clubs and are regarded by apartheid sports administrators in the same way as South African provincial teams.

6 REPRESSION

Namibia is ruled through force. In the northern half of the country and particularly in the northern bantustans where the South African military occupation is the most intense, troops and police have powers akin to martial law. People living in these areas, about 60 per cent of the population, face the constant threat of assault, detention without trial, torture or summary execution.[1] (The military aspect is dealt with in more detail in the following chapter.)

In the rest of the country, rule by the gun is less direct, but police and soldiers are always on hand to deal with resistance and enforce repressive laws.

The South African legal system and courts provide a veneer of legality for the ruthless suppression of opposition. Repressive South African 'security' laws have been imposed, along with proclamations which have given extensive and arbitrary powers to police and troops and severely restrict freedom of movement, residence, assembly and political organisation. The actions of the police and army are carried out under a cloak of secrecy and are indemnified in law.

REPRESSION THROUGH THE COURTS

A body of South African law, much of it aimed at eliminating resistance or controlling the black population, has been extended to Namibia. These laws include legislation drawn up for South Africa but applied also to Namibia, as well as specific measures applied only to Namibia. Repressive emergency regulations have also been imposed by proclamations, issued by the South African Administrator-General in the territory since 1977.

During periods in which South African-imposed administrations in Windhoek have been given some limited local authority (see Chapter 2) these administrations have imposed additional repressive measures.

The South African court system has also been extended to Namibia. As part of the process of conferring the appearance of limited autonomy on the Namibian administration, a Supreme Court was established in Windhoek in 1981. Appeals are referred to the Appellate Division of the South African Supreme Court in Bloemfontein. Less serious cases are dealt with by magistrates' courts. Judges and magistrates are appointed by the occupation authorities – there is no jury system.

> The institutions of the rule of law such as the Police, the courts, the legal practitioners and the law itself, are suspect in the eyes of the overwhelming majority of the people.
>
> *Bar Council of South-West Africa*

In the bantustans the authorities have appointed officials known as headmen or chiefs to administer civil and criminal law and impose fines or corporal punishment.[2] This is supposedly done 'in accordance with traditional law' but the powers exercised by these officials, and the way they exercise this authority to enforce apartheid laws, bears little resemblance to the system of justice which existed before colonialism. In the mid-1970s hundreds of SWAPO supporters and opponents of the bantustan authorities were subjected to public floggings under this system, many suffering serious injury.

Over the years the regime has widened its powers to deal with resistance. The legal rights of Namibians have been eroded to the extent that any Namibian may be detained indefinitely without trial, without any reason being provided by the administration and without access to lawyers or family.

REPRESSIVE LAWS

The UN Security Council and the International Court of Justice have repeatedly declared that the use of the courts for repressive purposes and the application of South African laws to Namibia is a violation of international law.

In 1970 the Security Council ruled that 'the extension and enforcement of South African laws in the territory together with the continued detentions, trials and subsequent sentencing of Namibians by the Government of South Africa constitute illegal acts and flagrant violations of the rights of the Namibians concerned, the Universal Declaration of Human Rights and the international status of the territory'.[3]

South African 'security' laws aimed at suppressing opposition have wide-ranging application.

The Terrorism Act, which was introduced in 1967, was applied in both South Africa and Namibia but was specifically aimed at dealing with the armed struggle launched by SWAPO in the previous year. It was rushed through the South African parliament and made retroactive to 1962 in order to try 37 Namibians who had already been arrested because of their suspected involvement in launching the armed struggle (see 'Political Prisoners' below).

The Terrorism Act provides for indefinite detention for the

purposes of interrogation. It establishes sentences up to the death sentence for 'terroristic acts', which are defined loosely and widely, including 'intent to endanger the maintenance of law and order'.

The Internal Security Act incorporates provisions of the 1950 Suppression of Communism Act, and was extended to Namibia in 1976. It is also wide-ranging, providing for the banning of organisations and the prohibition of meetings and political activities. Similar prohibitions can also be enforced through the Riotous Assemblies Act of 1956, which was extended to Namibia in 1976.

Further restrictive laws were introduced in 1985, just before the inauguration of the MPC administration. The Demonstrations in or near Court Buildings Prohibition Act, as its name implies, is used to prevent protests and demonstrations at trials. The Intimidation Act contains provisions for suppressing collective action such as strikes and boycotts. The Protection of Information Act imposes wide-ranging restrictions on information about military, police and government activities.[4]

In South Africa, such legislation was consolidated and strengthened through the adoption of an all-embracing Internal Security Act in 1982. A similar process was set in motion in Namibia in 1983 by the convening of the Van Dyk Commission of Inquiry into Security Legislation.

The Commission heard strong representations from the Namibian Bar Council for an end to detention without trial and the introduction of safeguards for detainees in order to inhibit torture. The Bar Council, which represents Namibian advocates and attorneys, also asked for an investigation into the activities of the army and police in torturing and intimidating civilians, and called for an end to the immunity from prosecution afforded to troops.

Police Task Force in Katutura

Plainclothes police break up SWAPO rally

Home destroyed by armoured vehicles

The Van Dyk Commission accepted that 'security' legislation infringed human rights, but stated that it was necessary in order to counter a 'revolutionary onslaught' in Namibia. Most of the recommendations of the Commission were made public at the end of 1986.[5]

In August 1988 the Protection of Fundamental Rights Act, closely patterned on State of Emergency regulations imposed in South Africa in June 1986, further increased police and army powers. Soldiers and police were empowered to 'enter and search any premises and to search, arrest and detain in custody any person'. The act also outlawed school and other boycotts and worker stay-aways by imposing sentences of up to ten years for calling for or participating in such protests. It was almost immediately used against boycotting students.

POLITICAL PRISONERS

Most repression bypasses the courts, and is carried out directly by the police and army. Namibians who do come to court face the full weight of a legal system aimed at securing convictions. Police interrogators use prolonged detention, usually in solitary confinement, to extort incriminating statements. Often detainees are tortured. At this stage detainees are denied access to lawyers and may make damaging admissions or plead guilty before receiving legal advice.

Witnesses for the prosecution are also detained and isolated for long periods. Evidence obtained through the prolonged interrogation of detainees has formed a large part of the prosecution's case in many political trials, and is usually accepted by the court even if denied by defendants during the trial. Pressure on detainees has resulted in cases where defendants have had to undergo psychiatric assessment during trials.

Thirty-seven Namibians were sentenced either to life imprisonment or 20 years under the Terrorism Act in 1968. They included Toivo ja Toivo, a founder of SWAPO, and many leading SWAPO members who had launched the movement's armed struggle. The trial, which took place in defiance of the UN Security Council and international protests, was held in Pretoria after the interrogation and lengthy torture of the accused.[6]

Further lengthy prison sentences were handed out to SWAPO members during the 1970s and 1980s. In 1976 two SWAPO leaders, Aaron Muchimba and Hendrik Shikongo, were sentenced to death for allegedly assisting guerrillas. Their convictions were overturned following strong international protests and an appeal which revealed that Security Police had infiltrated the office of the defence attorneys. A death sentence on a farm worker, Markus Kateka, which was imposed

NAMIBIAN POLITICAL PRISONERS

In addition to a fluctuating number of detainees held without trial, the following Namibians were imprisoned for political offences in July 1988.

Name	Date of Sentence	Length of Sentence	Act Offence
Markus KATEKA	13.10.80	17 years	Terrorism Act
Theofilus JASON	2.6.82	9 years	Terrorism Act
Josef SAGARIUS	2.6.82	9 years	Terrorism Act
Angula MWAALA	26.5.83	11 years	Common law (murder, robbery), Terrorism Act
Veiko Paulus NGHITEWA	30.10.85	24 years	Common law (murder, abduction, theft)
Sam MUNDJINDJI	30.10.85	24 years	Common law (murder, abduction, theft)
Frans ANGULA	7.5.86	16 years	Terrorism Act
Norbert ANKOME	7.5.86	14 years	Terrorism Act
Elkan Simon SHOOMBE	7.5.86	14 years	Terrorism Act
Desiderius ANKOME	7.5.86	12 years	Terrorism Act
Erastus UUTONI	7.5.86	12 years	Terrorism Act
Vilho KASHILULU	7.5.86	12 years	Terrorism Act
Bernadinus Petrus SHIKONKO	7.5.86	5 years	Terrorism Act
Paulus KAPUMBURU	Aug. 86	12 years	Common law (murder)
Leonard NAFTALI	28.11.86	18 years	Common law (murder)
Jonas HINGASHEPUA	17.2.87	12 years & 6 mnths	GLA (sabotage)
Evans Salwindi SIMASIKU	12.5.87	10 years	GLA (sabotage)
Andreas Johnny HEITA	22.5.87	18 years	Terrorism Act
Johannes NANGOLO	22.5.87	12 years	Possession of explosives
Martin AKWEENDA	22.5.87	10 years	Terrorism Act
Gabriel MATEUS	22.5.87	8 years	Possession of explosives
Salomo PAULUS	22.5.87	7 years	Terrorism Act
Gabriel NDAPUKA	27.5.87	3 years	GLA (sabotage)

GLA = General Law Amendment Act

We are Namibians and not South Africans. We do not now, and will not in the future recognize your right to govern us; to make laws for us in which we had no say; to treat our country as if you were our masters.

We have always regarded South Africa as an intruder in our country. This is how we have always felt and this is how we feel now, and it is on this basis that we have faced this trial . . .

We know that our organisation, SWAPO, is the largest political organization in South West Africa. We consider ourselves a political party. We know that whites do not think of blacks as politicians – only as agitators. Many of our people, through no fault of their own, have had no education at all. This does not mean they do not know what they want.

A man does not have to be formally educated to know that he wants to live with his family where he wants to live, and not where an official chooses to tell him to live; to move about freely and not require a pass; to earn a decent wage; to be free to work for the person of his choice for as long as he wants; and finally, to be ruled by the people that he wants to be ruled by, and not those who rule him because they have more guns than he has . . .

Andimba Toivo ja Toivo, court statement, 1968

Andimba Toivo ja Toivo

Windhoek prison

in 1980 was also overturned following an international campaign.[7]

Many Namibian political prisoners have been kept in gaols in South Africa, especially on Robben Island near Cape Town. Toivo ja Toivo and others were imprisoned there together with Nelson Mandela and other ANC leaders. All Namibian political prisoners are now held in prisons in Namibia.

Prison conditions are harsh – the diet for black prisoners is bad and bedding and other facilities are inadequate. Many political prisoners have been beaten or subjected to harsh work discipline, especially those who were imprisoned on Robben Island. They have suffered psychological torture, been denied reading material and cut off from contact with the outside world.[8]

During 1984 and 1985 Toivo ja Toivo, Eliazer Tuhadaleni, Immanuel Shifidi, Ben Ulenga, John Pandeni and other long-term political prisoners were released, in a move seen as an attempt to give credibility to the new MPC administration. However, not all Namibian political prisoners were released, and subsequent trials of SWAPO supporters resulted in long prison sentences of up to 24 years.

The torture of detainees revealed in trials during 1986 and 1987 showed that the pattern of torturing detainees to extract 'confessions' had changed little since the first trial under the Terrorism Act twenty years previously.[9]

On the same day we were sentenced, 9 February 1968, we were taken by truck to Robben Island. We were made to strip naked and then we were given prison clothes. We were not given shoes.

One morning we were taken to a dumping ground where we were ordered to clean up the rubbish. This went on for about a week. Afterwards we were ordered to clear the dry branches in the wood on Robben Island. At first the warders were reluctant to give us axes, so for three weeks we just broke the wood with our bare hands.

We were also ordered to work in the quarry, which we found very difficult because the stone was white and it became dazzling. It was hard to work with just picks, shovels and spades, and we did not have anything to protect our eyes from the glare. We couldn't see properly. As a result most of our people now have to wear dark glasses.

In 1971 we gave a representative from the International Red Cross some of our complaints. Afterwards we were beaten up. Two of my comrades were locked up and denied food without any explanation. So we went on a hunger strike. In the middle of the night we just heard dogs barking in the passages. Doors were thrown open and five or six warders were ordered into each cell. They ordered us to strip naked and stand against the wall with our arms stretched high and our legs outstretched. They rained blows on us with batons and truncheons. Some of us were badly beaten. The next morning we tried to consult a doctor, but we were refused permission to see him for a fortnight until our wounds were healed.

Helao Shityuwete, imprisoned on Robben Island, 1968-84

BANNING AND RESTRICTIONS ON MEETINGS

Some Namibians detained under Proclamation AG26 *(see 'Detention without Trial' below)* have been released under stringent restrictions. These have included house arrest during the hours of darkness, restriction to a certain area, prohibitions on meeting more than one or two people at a time, and prohibitions on teaching or being employed in the public sector.

Between 1968 and 1985 the Acting President of SWAPO, Nathaniel Maxuilili, was restricted to the Kuisebmond township in Walvis Bay and prohibited from addressing meetings or being quoted.[10]

Public activities such as political meetings are controlled by a number of measures. In the northern bantustans meetings are prohibited by the emergency regulations and SWAPO has been prevented from holding any public events there. In 1981 the Prohibition of Meetings Act was introduced, requiring organisers of meetings to obtain a permit. Until 1986 SWAPO was prevented from holding any public meetings under this Act – gatherings were broken up and organisers arrested. Meetings may also be prevented under the Riotous Asssemblies Act and through municipal regulations. These restrictions have made open political organisation very difficult.[11]

DETENTION WITHOUT TRIAL

Proclamations or emergency regulations issued by the South African head of state or his local agents complement 'security' laws as repressive measures, and are the main measures used by troops and police to detain and intimidate people in the war zones.

Proclamation AG26, the Detention for the Prevention of Political Violence and Intimidation Proclamation, was introduced in 1978 and has been used throughout Namibia mainly to detain SWAPO leaders. Deten-

Ida Jimmy, chairperson of SWAPO Women's Council, was sentenced to seven years in prison – reduced on appeal to five – for calling for support for SWAPO fighters at a public meeting. She was seven months pregnant at the time.

It was a very difficult time because when I was arrested on 15 October 1980 I was kept in solitary confinement. There was no family contact and no contact with the rest of the prisoners. When you are held like that on your own, totally isolated, you wonder all the time what is going to happen to you.

A baby boy, Konjeleni Richard, was born on 17 December 1980 but with some complications and he had to be kept in an incubator. They took me to the clinic and there I was kept for three days. When I came back from the clinic I had to continue the work I left behind. I was not strong enough but I tried to continue with the duties of a prisoner which I was compelled to do. If you do not fulfil the requirements of the duties then you do not get any food. As a mother who had to breast feed it was important for me to eat.

It is a difficult experience one has in the Central Prison of Windhoek. Not only the political prisoners experience real difficulties but all prisoners. If you are ill you do not get any immediate medical help from a doctor. You can stay as long as three days without any medical assistance . . .

After 18 months my child was taken away from me . . . Then I had to contact someone to take the child, because I knew nobody in Windhoek and Luderitz is nearly 800 kilometres from the Windhoek prison. I asked them to contact my mother to come and take the child and they told me that my mother refused to take a child of a political prisoner. That was not the truth.

The boy was looked after by Ida Jimmy's mother, but died a year later. She was refused permission to attend his funeral.

tions are carried out on the orders of the authorities in Windhoek for 'preventive' reasons and those detained may be held indefinitely.[12]

The Security Districts Proclamation, AG9 of 1977, replaced emergency regulations which had been imposed in the early 1970s in the Ovambo, Kavango and Eastern Caprivi bantustans. Since 1979 many of the provisions of AG9 have been enforced in Windhoek and most of the districts to the north of the capital.[13]

The restrictive scope of AG9 has been progressively extended through successive amendments since 1978. It empowers police and troops to detain individuals for interrogation for 30 days without reference to any higher authority – this can be extended indefinitely with the authorisation of the central administration.

Detainees may be held incommunicado without access to lawyers or relatives, although lawyers have access after 30 days of detention. The police or military authorities are not required to disclose who is being detained, or where they are held, or even to inform relatives.[14]

It is not known how many people are held at any one time under AG9. SADF units regularly detain people without reporting this to sector headquarters.

When giving evidence to the Van Dyk Commission of Inquiry into Security Legislation the military authorities were unable to provide a figure for the number of people they had detained. They had records of 2,883 people who had been detained between 1977 and 1983, but admitted that many more had not been recorded. Not one of the people detained by them had been charged with any offence.

For the same period, the Security Police disclosed that they had detained 2,624 people, 90 per cent of whom were not subsequently charged.[15]

Only in rare cases is detention a prelude to trial. It is used primarily for interrogation and intimidation and to remove activists from their communities, as part of South Africa's

61

THE KASSINGA DETAINEES

On 4 May 1978 South African troops carried out an airborne attack on a SWAPO refugee camp at Kassinga in Angola. Over 700 refugees were killed and between 200 and 300 captured and taken back to Namibia.

The prisoners were interrogated under torture at Oshakati military base. Electric shocks, beatings and suspension were the techniques of torture most widely used. Sixty-three of the detainees were released on 27 May.

A year later the names of 130 captives still being detained, a third of them women, were made public by UN officials. The South African authorities denied the existence of the Kassinga detainees.

In January 1980 the International Red Cross reported that 118 Kassinga survivors were being detained under Proclamation AG9 at the Keikamachab detention camp at Hardap Dam near Mariental in central Namibia.

An international campaign was mounted to secure the release of the detainees, and in 1984 relatives and three Namibian bishops brought an action in the Windhoek Supreme Court for the release of 37 named detainees. Invoking powers under the Defence Act, the South African State President banned the court action.

Following strong international protests, the Kassinga detainees were released later in 1984. Those detained revealed that they had all been tortured and interrogated at Oshakati, and then held under harsh conditions at Keikamachab camp. They had been forced to carry out labouring tasks and had been assaulted on a number of occasions. Throughout the period, they had been denied visits from their families or access to lawyers.

Refugees abducted from Kassinga

One of two mass graves at Kassinga, May 1978

efforts to maintain control and fight SWAPO. Many, perhaps most, of the thousands who have been detained have been tortured.[16]

At times, hundreds of people have been rounded up in mass detentions, while many detainees have been held secretly and without access to the outside world for years. For example, information about the detention of an individual in 1985 only came to light three years later. Many Namibians have simply disappeared, presumed abducted by the South African armed forces.

Over 140 people were detained for six years at a detention centre near Mariental – they were captured by the SADF during an attack on the Kassinga refugee camp in Angola in 1978. Detentions have also been used in an attempt to immobilise SWAPO inside Namibia – at some critical periods most of the leadership has been held without trial.[17]

THE PERSECUTION OF AXEL JOHANNES

Axel Johannes, for several years SWA-PO's Administrative Secretary in Namibia, bears visible marks of repeated torture by the South African police. By the time he left Namibia in 1980, aged 35, he had spent nearly one-third of his life in prison or detention without charge. His case history is a striking illustration of the persistent harassment and intimidation to which SWAPO leaders are subjected.

Axel Johannes joined SWAPO in 1959 as a teenager. He was arrested in 1964 and again in 1966, when he was held in solitary confinement along with Toivo ja Toivo and other SWAPO leaders.

His third detention occurred in 1973 under Proclamation R17 through which a state of emergency had been imposed in the north following the 1971-2 contract workers' strike. He was detained for more than three months.

In January 1974 he was again arrested, together with other SWAPO leaders, and held in solitary confinement under the Terrorism Act for six months. He was repeatedly tortured.

In August 1975 Johannes was arrested in Windhoek and detained incommunicado for seven months. He was again tortured and assaulted. In March the following year he was brought before the court to give evidence against SWAPO members accused of the assassination of a bantustan official. He refused, and was imprisoned for a year. On his release, he was immediately detained under the Terrorism Act.

He was again arrested at the end of 1977 for refusing to give evidence against a fellow SWAPO member charged under the Terrorism Act, and was fined.

In April 1978 he was rearrested in the course of country-wide police operations against SWAPO, and was released in October after being repeatedly tortured.

After less than six weeks of liberty, he was arrested with 85 other SWAPO members, assaulted and held until Christmas that year.

In February 1979 Johannes travelled to the north of Namibia to visit his parents, whom he had not seen for two years. He was detained by police, assaulted and subjected to electric shock torture. He was eventually found guilty of violating the curfew and fined.

In April that year another extended period of detention commenced, after his return from consultations with the UN in New York. Along with 50 other SWAPO members he was held incommunicado in solitary confinement, until his release at the end of July.

He was then subjected to virtual house arrest, forbidden to leave Katutura township and restricted to his house between 8 p.m. and 6 a.m. He was not allowed to receive visitors, have anyone else in the house, or take up employment. At the end of 1980 he was allowed to leave Namibia.

In the northern bantustans, the provisions of Proclamation AG9 extend far beyond detention without trial. Troops and police are empowered to search vehicles or buildings, impound property and enforce curfews and restrictions on meetings or the movement or residence of people.

The South African Administrator-General issued a number of proclamations declaring the northern bantustans to be 'prohibited areas' and preventing people from entering or leaving them without police or military permits. This was extended to the bantustans of Hereroland East and Bushmanland in 1986. The restrictions were lifted at the end of 1987 on the grounds that they were ineffective, and there were reports that new measures were being considered.[18]

Strict dusk-to-dawn curfews have been imposed in terms of Proclamation AG9 in the northern bantustans since the early 1970s , especially in Ovambo. These prevent people from leaving the confines of their homesteads, although the boundaries of homesteads are not defined and the various parts of a homestead are often spread over a wide area.

The dusk-to-dawn curfew regulation in northern Namibia has once again claimed the life of a young man, and has left two other people with serious injuries after Koevoet members emptied their magazines into a light pick-up van with four occupants last Friday.

Survivor Jacob Muhongo told *The Namibian* that he and his three friends were returning home from Eenhana, and that they were driving slowly as they were already near their home.

'It was just past eight in the evening, when suddenly, without any warning we found ourselves under heavy attack from nearby. It was clear that Koevoet was shooting to kill, for they were aiming at the total area of the vehicle.'

The Namibian, *29.1.88*

Ida Jimmy, SWAPO leader, on her release from prison

A person abroad after dark in the region is liable to be challenged by Security Force patrols, and Security Force members generally do not speak the indigenous languages, nor are many local residents fluent in English or Afrikaans.

The process of being challenged often occurs in inherently dangerous circumstances of surprise, limited visibility and varying conditions of audibility.

A response by civilians to the military challenge adjudged unsatisfactory may lead to apprehension, imprisonment, interrogation and prosecution, or to death or injury by shooting.

Application by three Namibian bishops to the Supreme Court for the curfew to be set aside

The enforcement of the curfew is determined by local military commanders. Police and soldiers have revealed in court that their orders are to 'shoot anything that moves' after sunset, and there have been numerous cases where civilians have been killed for moving about at night, often on their own property. In some cases people seeking urgent medical attention at night have been shot. In other cases people have been shot while going to the toilet, or looking after livestock on their property.[19]

TORTURE

Many Namibians have made affidavits or statements testifying to being tortured by the army or police, and church and other sources in touch with the war zones have repeatedly stated that torture of detainees is routine.

Troops and police use torture as a means of obtaining information from people suspected of knowing about SWAPO activities and as part of the overall process of intimidation and terrorisation to dissuade people from supporting SWAPO. Torture is applied widely in the war zones, and beatings form part of normal day-to-day operations by troops and police.

The Southern African Catholic Bishops Conference reported in 1982: 'That detention and interrogation in any part of the country are accompanied by beating, torture, spare diet and solitary confinement is accepted as common knowledge'.[20]

A similar conclusion was drawn by the British Council of Churches in 1981 after a delegation had visited Namibia and heard evidence of at least twenty cases of torture and other abuses carried out by the 'security forces' in the six weeks before their visit.[21]

A black policeman came with a rope, tied my arms behind my back and blindfolded me, then electricity was attached to the little fingers of both my hands. It was switched on and off and I screamed . . . This started from eight in the morning until two o'clock.

The following morning again I was brought to a small room. A rope was tied around my neck and pulled. I fell down unconscious. When I woke up I was in a pool of blood and realised that I had broken my jaw and blood was running. I asked for a doctor but I was told I was not going to be given one until I told the truth . . .

This time I was tortured from 8 o'clock in the morning until 12 noon. In the afternoon I was taken back to the office and a small chain that looked like a necklace was put around my neck. My whole neck started itching so terribly that I thought it was going to be cut off.

This went on until after three o'clock the following afternoon, then I was sent back to my cell just to be collected the following morning. Then they started with their electrical instruments; this time it was administered on my breasts. It went on for almost three hours. After that I was ordered to stand without making any movement.

Rauna Nambinga, describing her torture in Oshakati prison in 1980

Police in armoured vehicles, Windhoek, 1988

Detainees are commonly kept in corrugated-iron 'cages' at interrogation centres near military or police bases. They are often denied food or water and kept for long periods in solitary confinement.

The police blindfolded me again and took me to the room where they torture people. They took all my clothes off me so that I was just left with my underwear on. Then they tied me up by my arms. My feet were three or four feet from the ground.

They put ice in my mouth and on top of it some kind of plug. I think it was one of those things they use in mental hospitals. I felt somebody putting a string round both my thumbs and tying it very tight. I was still blindfolded but I could feel somebody tying my ears and my big toes – both of them. After that I felt something being put in my vagina...

Suddenly the whole of the left side of my body started to ache. It was very, very painful. I don't know what they did to me. Then they started on the other side. After this they did both sides at the same time. I think that it was electric shock, but I don't really know. It hurt so badly that I lost consciousness.

Later I woke up and saw that I was lying on the floor with absolutely no clothes on me. Somebody was pouring iced water all over my body. One policeman kicked me and said that I must walk to my cell. I could not stand up. I just had to crawl. They put my dress on me and from there they took me to my cell.

Within a few minutes I saw that I was bleeding . . . I was three and a half months pregnant.

I bled for eight days alone in my cell. The police refused to take me to the doctor. They just left me there. On the ninth day they came to take me to the army doctor. He had come to my cell once before and given me aspirin. This time he told me that I had some kind of infection. I told him: 'I do not have an infection, I was pregnant' . . .

From there I was taken back to my cell where I stayed for a further six days without treatment. On the seventh day the police came to fetch me again for more torture.

Magdalena, victim of torture (quoted in Allison, 1986)

Methods of torture which have been repeatedly reported include being beaten, deprived of sleep, buried in holes in the ground, forced under water, strangled, suffocated, suspended from poles or ropes, held over fires, threatened with death and being shown corpses, threatened with snakes, subjected to electric shocks to various parts of the body including the genitals and being held against the hot exhausts of military vehicles.[22]

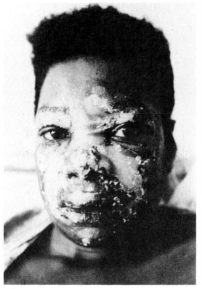

13-year-old Portas Blasius, tortured by being held against the exhaust of a military vehicle

14-year-old schoolgirl beaten by police, August 1988

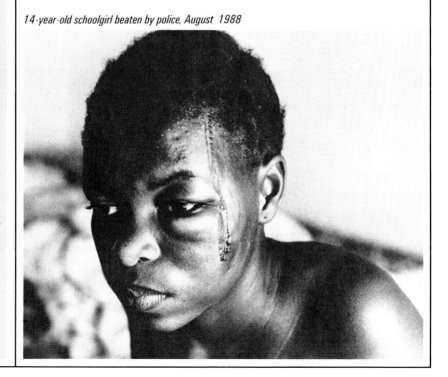

A cowering and fearful 13-year-old girl told of how she had been beaten and given electric shocks by a band of marauding soldiers in northern Namibia.

She said that on Tuesday night of this week three army Buffels, packed with soldiers and each commanded by a white man, had stopped at the homestead of Mr Abraham Moses, 60, where the young Line was then visiting with her mother.

The soldiers proceeded to forcefully question them about the movements of SWAPO guerrillas who had allegedly been active in the Ongandjera area the night before. During the questioning they ordered the elderly Mr Moses out of the house, and told his wife to remain inside while 'we kill your husband outside'.

They had then allegedly assaulted the old man, fired shots into the air apparently to frighten his wife who was still inside the house, and then gave him electric shocks with a device they took from the Buffel armoured car.

Line then said that they had then turned on her, holding her while giving her electric shocks on her hands.

The Namibian, *7.8.87*

According to the Namibian Bar Council, only a few of the many incidents of torture ever reach the courts. Those reporting torture are likely to face further detention or other reprisals, and the courts usually dismiss evidence of torture during trials.

The South African regime has ignored the accusations or dismissed them as 'SWAPO propaganda'.

> You thrash him until he cracks, until he points out what has to be pointed out.
>
> . . . He told lies . . . but after being assaulted he was completely willing to tell the truth.
>
> . . . I gave the man what we can term a good hiding.
>
> *Police officers describing torture of detainees in court, 1987*

In cases where prosecutions have been brought against members of the 'security forces', the punishment is often derisory. For example, two policemen who were found guilty of 'roasting' Ndara Kapitango, a 63-year-old man who suffered serious burns and eventually died of his injuries, were each fined R50.[23] *(See also 'Intimidation and Brutality' in Chapter 7)*

Farmworker Kasire Thomas, pictured just before his death, chained and forced to make a clenched-fist salute during torture by his employer

DISAPPEARANCES AND EXECUTIONS

The system of widespread secret detention accompanied by torture creates conditions in which extra-judicial executions may be carried out by police or soldiers. In several cases, people detained by the 'security forces' have not been seen again by their relatives.

Hundreds of people have disappeared without trace from the war zones or been killed and buried without inquests being carried out. When inquests are held, they are often cursory and blame is ascribed to 'persons unknown' or to 'unidentified terrorists'. Local people disbelieve many of these inquests and blame the killings on the police or army – there are cases where police or army units have deliberately disguised their killing as the work of SWAPO *(see Chapter 7)*.

In 1985 inquests into the violent deaths of 600 Namibians were heard in the Ondangua magistrates' court – most of these were attributed to unknown or unidentified persons.[24]

It is common practice for troops to leave the bodies of their victims where they lie, and inquests are not usually carried out. Units responsible for much of the fighting, like the Koevoet Police Counter-Insurgency Unit, do not keep formal records of their killings. This makes it easy to disguise the murder of civilians as the death of 'enemy' personnel in combat.[25]

Little is known of the fate of captured SWAPO fighters. SADF reports of clashes hardly ever indicate the capture or wounding of guerrillas, even where large numbers are reported to have been killed. The International Red Cross has expressed concern about the fate of captured SWAPO fighters, noting in 1981 that 'it simply does not happen in any conflict or battle that you have a clash with 200 people and 45 killed and no prisoners or wounded are taken'.[26]

South African troops display corpses of their victims

Ndara Kapitango, roasted alive by police

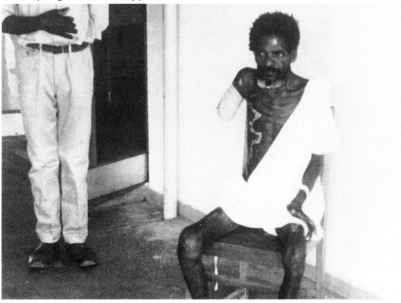

From available evidence it appears that guerrillas who are captured are either killed after being interrogated, or are imprisoned in 'cages' and tortured, mainly in the Oshakati and Ondangua detention centres. Some captured combatants are persuaded by torture and threats against their families to join the South African armed forces.

Relatively few SWAPO fighters have been charged in the courts. Death sentences and long prison terms have been handed out after such trials. The South African regime does not recognise the entitlement of SWAPO combatants to prisoner-of-war status. Under a 1977 protocol, the Geneva Conventions on the rules of war were extended to anti-colonial struggles and wars of 'national liberation or self-determination'. Under this protocol SWAPO fighters should be entitled to the rights of prisoners of war and SWAPO has itself endorsed the protocol. The South African regime has also systematically violated the provisions of the Geneva Conventions governing the treatment of civilians.[27]

7 MILITARY OCCUPATION

Tens of thousands of troops and police maintain the South African occupation of Namibia. Especially in the north, where martial law is in force, the activities of the army overshadow the lives of civilians, who live in fear of detention, beatings or death.

Namibia is one of the most militarised countries in the world. It is not possible to calculate accurately the fluctuating number of troops in the territory and the South African authorities do not issue comprehensive figures. One widely used estimate is 100,000 occupation troops, including locally recruited forces.[1]

Military bases are scattered throughout the territory, and in many parts the army is the only source of employment. Towns such as Grootfontein, Ondangua and Oshakati have become military garrisons and in Windhoek the army has taken over many buildings.

South African troops control health, recreational and educational facilities in some bantustans. In an attempt to gain the support of Namibians – to 'win hearts and minds' – the army distributes dozens of free propaganda publications and has set up propaganda organisations which promote allegiance to the occupation forces under the guise of 'culture'.[2]

The military authorities play a vital role in the administration of the territory. Decisions about Namibia are taken in Pretoria's military-dominated State Security Council and the South African Minister of Defence usually takes part in major discusssions about the future of the territory.[3]

THE WAR

The struggle in Namibia is referred to by the South African authorities as a 'low intensity guerrilla war', but the large number of troops involved and the extensive militarisation of the territory belies the description. The South African occupation has exacted a tremendous toll on Namibia – at least an estimated 10,000 dead, tens of thousands exiled or made homeless, and incalculable damage to Namibian society.[4]

Today the occupation of Namibia accounts for more than a tenth of the South African government budget, and up to half the army's mobilised strength has been committed to the war in Namibia and Angola. Despite this, SWAPO's People's Liberation Army of Namibia (PLAN), has sustained and expanded its armed struggle for more than twenty years.[5]

In the first phase of the war, from 1966 to 1972, guerrilla activities were limited mainly to the north-east in the Caprivi Strip, and South African police were responsible for combating PLAN. As documented in Chapter 3, the workers' strike of 1971-2 led thousands of Namibians to join SWAPO, and the war soon spread through the populous north.

The collapse of Portuguese colonialism in Angola in 1975 led to independence for that

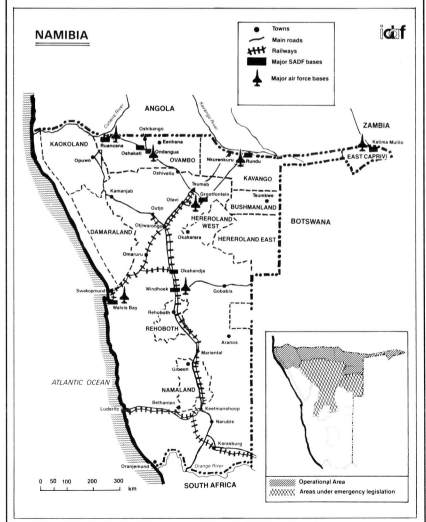

NAMIBIA

- Towns
- Main roads
- Railways
- Major SADF bases
- Major air force bases

idaf

ANGOLA

ZAMBIA

Cunene River

Kavango River

Oshikango

KAOKOLAND

Ruancana   Eenhana

Opuwo   Oshakati   Ondangua

OVAMBO

Katima Mulilo

EAST CAPRIVI

Nkurenkuru   Rundu

Oshivello

KAVANGO

Kamanjab

Tsumeb

Otavi   Grootfontein   Tsumkwe

Outjo   BUSHMANLAND

Otjiwarongo   HEREROLAND WEST

DAMARALAND   Okakarara   BOTSWANA

HEREROLAND EAST

Omaruru

Okahandja

Swakopmund   Windhoek   Gobabis

Walvis Bay

Rehoboth

REHOBOTH

Aranos

Mariental

ATLANTIC OCEAN

Gibeon

NAMALAND

Bethanien

Luderitz   Keetmanshoop

Narubis

Karasburg

Oranjemund   Orange River

0 50 100   200   300

km

SOUTH AFRICA

Operational Area
Areas under emergency legislation

country under the MPLA liberation movement, which was committed to supporting SWAPO. The whole of northern Namibia was thus opened up for PLAN operations. Thousands of South African conscripts were sent to the north, and the current phase of intensified guerrilla warfare set in. Since then hardly a day has passed without conflict between the occupation forces and PLAN.

The northern bantustans, where over half the Namibian population lives, are the SADF's 'operational area'. The area is peppered with military and police bases, ranging from small platoon-strength temporary bases to large garrisons like Oshakati.

From their bases troops carry out patrols on foot or in armoured vehicles or on horses or motor cycles, scouring the bush for signs of PLAN activity. Guerrillas, usually operating in small groups, sabotage military and strategic targets, lay ambushes for army patrols and attack bases at night. Early each year, during the rainy season when the vegetation is denser and provides better cover, groups of combatants move south towards the militarised white farming areas.

Sabotage operations are carried out throughout Namibia, including in and near the main urban centres, but most of the fighting occurs in the Ovambo bantustan, where the relatively dense rural population provides PLAN with a strong support base.

Provided with food and shelter by local people, small numbers of PLAN fighters are able to tie down tens of thousands of South African troops. The SADF has resorted to the widespread intimidation of the local population, forcibly moved villages from some areas of intense guerrilla activity, depopulated the key area along the Angola border with the Ovambo bantustan, and tried to destroy and control crops and food and water supplies in an attempt to deny the guerrillas their support from the local population.

During the 1980s the SADF's strategy has shifted from an emphasis on infantry patrols to fight the guerillas, to using units like Koevoet Police Counter-Insurgency Unit, which rely on the mobility and firepower of their armoured vehicles in combat situation.[6] *(The armed struggle is examined in more detail in the following chapter.)*

Government building at Oluno, northern Namibia, sabotaged by PLAN

Police patrol in Bushmanland bantustan

KOEVOET (COIN)

The COIN unit has a strength of over a thousand, mostly black Namibian police recruited from the ranks of the Special Constables and commanded by white South African police or mercenaries, many of whom are ex-members of the Rhodesian Selous Scouts.

If the presence of guerrillas is detected, trackers follow the trail while the main body of the COIN unit follows in Casspir armoured vehicles. The unit keeps no records of the people it kills. A commander has admitted that 'We are not interested in captures. Killing is the name of the game.' Members of the COIN unit receive *'kopgeld'* (Afrikaans for 'head money') for every killing they carry out, amounting to up to three times their monthly salary. The unit is widely feared in the northern areas of Namibia and has been accused of widespread terror and intimidation. A number of Koevoet members have been found responsible for torturing and killing civilians.

Extract from Focus, *No 61, November-December 1985*

FORCES OF OCCUPATION

Thousands of white South African conscript troops are sent to Namibia every year. They are stationed in the territory for periods of up to eighteen months during their initial two-year stint of compulsory military service and may return subsequently on three-month operational deployments. Smaller numbers of South African police are also dispatched to the territory, serving mainly in a military capacity in the north.

Conscripts make up the bulk of the South African army's mechanised conventional-warfare units based in Namibia, which are used mainly for invasions of Angola. More than 2,000 troops are also stationed in the Walvis Bay Military Area, which is used for training and encloses a naval and air base.[7]

Many of the South African conscript troops spend their time at rear bases or on routine bush patrols. Much of the fighting is borne by Namibian-manned units (see below). Follow-up operations against SWAPO guerrillas are usually carried out by 'reaction forces' attached to the northern bases, or by special combat units such as Koevoet. These professional units have gained notoriety for their brutal methods.[8]

SWA TERRITORY FORCE

Since 1974 the South Africans have been recruiting black Namibians into the occupation army. Recruitment generally takes place in rural areas, where military service – which offers high salaries by Namibian standards – is often the only alternative to poverty and unemployment.

Several segregated units have been set up in different bantustans, some of which have more than 2,000 troops. A large force of black auxiliary 'Special Constables' has also been formed, mainly to guard bantustan leaders.

White men, especially farmers, are organised into local part-time Area Force Units. These units back up the regular forces and carry out routine patrolling and guard duties. Most farmers are armed and maintain radio contact with military bases, acting as a 'first line of defence' outside the bantustans.

All white Namibian males are conscripted in the same way as their South African counterparts for two years' full-time training and service followed by twelve years of part-time duties. Since 1981 conscription has been imposed on black Namibian men living outside the northern bantustans.

Religious, community and student organisations have fiercely resisted military service. Thousands of people have left Namibia to avoid conscription and individuals have challenged the regime's right to conscript them.

Namibian-manned units have been separated administratively into the South West Africa Territory Force (SWATF), which consists of about 20,000 troops, more than half of whom are black. As well as the bantustan units and Area Force Units, SWATF has a mechanised 'reaction force' mainly based near Windhoek, and runs a junior officer training school at Okahandja.

SWATF nominally falls under the Windhoek administration, but Pretoria exercises direct authority over all military operations in the territory and SWATF is in effect an arm of the SADF. The SWA Police force (SWAPOL) is similarly an extension of the South African Police.[9]

Police on family picnic in northern Namibia

INTIMIDATION AND BRUTALITY

South Africa's military occupation relies on force and terror. Atrocities have mounted with the intensification of the war. In the mid-1970s, when SWAPO's political and military mobilisation took deep root in the north, the SADF and its auxiliary forces mounted a terror campaign, rounding up thousands of people for interrogation.[10]

Katutura, 1988

The Security Forces stop at nothing to force information out of people. They break into homes, beat up residents, shoot people, steal and kill cattle and often pillage stores and tea rooms.

When the tracks of SWAPO guerrillas are discovered by the Security Forces the local people are in danger. Harsh measures are intensified. People are blindfolded, taken from their homes and left beaten up and even dead by the roadside. Women are often raped . . .

There is no redress because reporting irregularities or atrocities to commanders is considered a dangerous or fruitless exercise . . . A dusk to dawn curfew is imposed in the operational area. Anybody moving after dark is shot.

Southern African Catholic Bishops Conference, Report on Namibia, 1982

Torture has been institutionalised as a method of interrogation – it is clear from court evidence and official statements that it is sanctioned by military and police commanders.

Civilians suspected of aiding SWAPO are tortured for information on the whereabouts of guerrillas, while captured PLAN fighters, or people suspected of being PLAN members, are tortured for military intelligence purposes.[11]

Intimidation through terror, to dissuade local people from supporting SWAPO, is widespread. Troops select homesteads or settlements where people are thought to support the liberation struggle and carry out beatings or shootings. Sometimes these attacks are mounted secretly at night, or by troops disguised as

PLAN fighters, in attempts to discredit SWAPO. Koevoet specialises in such 'pseudo-guerrilla' operations.[12]

Soldiers have destroyed property, housing and crops in the war zones on a wide scale. Residents have repeatedly complained about armoured vehicles deliberately being driven through crops and fences, and homesteads are often burnt down in reprisal attacks. One reason for these attacks is to destroy the ability of local people to feed themselves and to support guerrillas, instead forcing them into dependency on the occupation forces.[13]

The occupation by the South African Defence Force in the name of 'protecting' the people of Namibia is causing hardship, distress, fear and loss of life. This is especially so in the north near the border with Angola where the people are caught in the crossfire between the SADF and SWAPO . . .

The curfew in operation in the north, the undoubted intimidation, the destruction of property, the restriction of movement, the spreading of distrust through informers, the divisions in family life, the cases of abduction, torture and beatings, the total massive armed presence of the SADF, cause the community to live in a state of perpetual fear and suspicion. The people fear the army and the Koevoet far more than they fear SWAPO.

Report to the Archbishop of Canterbury by an Anglican delegation after their visit of October 1983

Our main job is to take an area and clear it. We sweep through it and we kill everything in front of us, cattle, goats, people, everything. We are out to stop SWAPO and so we stop them getting into the villages for food and water.

Some of it is pretty heavy. Sometimes we take the locals for questioning. It's rough. We just beat them, cut them, burn them. As soon as we're finished with them we kill them.

Trevor Edwards, a British mercenary with the SADF's 32 Battalion describing operations in southern Angola in 1980

The enforcement of the night curfew is a major cause of civilian deaths in the war zones. Troops are under orders to shoot on sight anyone out after dark (*see previous chapter*).

As well as officially sanctioned terror, thousands of assaults, rapes, robberies and killings have been carried out by soldiers or police acting without official authorisation. There have been many cases of shootings carried out by off-duty police or troops, often after they have been drinking.

Rape and sexual assault on women is common. In some instances the perpetrators are brought before the courts, where they are usually given light sentences or small fines.

Cases brought before the courts represent only a small fraction of violent incidents. Victims of assault or rape are often frightened of reprisals and see little point in reporting attacks to

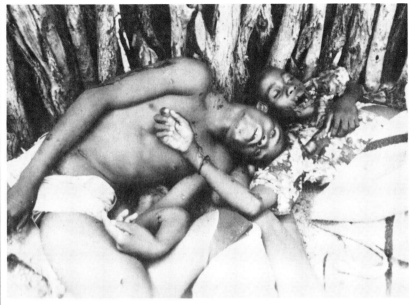

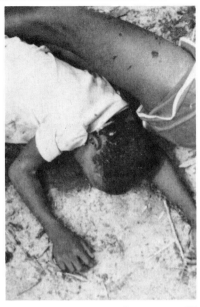

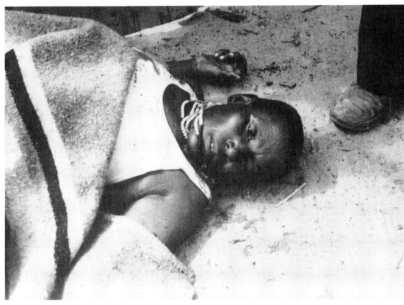

Reports about a massacre in a small village in the north of Namibia have thrown light on the key role of the paramilitary police unit Koevoet in carrying out atrocities while disguised as SWAPO guerrillas. Eyewitness accounts of the massacre, which took place on 10 March 1982 at the village of Oshipanda near Oshikuku in Ovambo, sharply contradict the finding of the inquest held in the Ondangua Inquest Court in June, which ruled that 'terrorists' were liable for the death of eight people murdered in the incident.

Extract from Focus, *IDAF Bulletin, November-December 1982, reporting local people's testimony that soldiers had lined villagers up against a wall and shot them with automatic weapons*

authorities closely identified with military structures. Troops can be granted immunity from prosecution. For example in March 1988 South African State President Botha invoked the Defence Act to halt the trial of six soldiers charged with murdering SWAPO leader Immanuel Slifidi.[14]

A 65-year-old Lutheran pastor who had been beaten up by South African Defence Force soldiers in April has died in hospital, apparently as a result of the assault. The head of the Lutheran church in northern Namibia, Bishop Kleopas Dumeni, has blamed the soldiers for his death.

Namibia Communications Centre, 30.7.87

In 1985, following growing criticism, military commanders issued a statement claiming that all 'transgressions' were punished. They provided a list of troops who had been fined or imprisoned for assault, rape and murder. However, these represented only a small proportion of reported incidents, and the punishments were often shockingly lenient. A Namibian lawyer, Anton Lubowski, has estimated that between only 10 and 20 per cent of violent cases have ever been brought to public attention.[15]

'HEARTS AND MINDS'

While the SADF relies on terror and force to combat SWAPO, it also emphasises the need to win popular support.

South African commanders stress that military operations must be carried out forcefully and decisively, but they should be accompanied by social, psychological and economic measures to 'pacify' the local population and remove the source of conflict. This is expressed in a dictum widely used in the SADF that the war is 80 per cent social or political and only 20 per cent military.[16]

Psychological warfare to 'win hearts and minds' is widely employed by the occupation troops. At its simplest, this involves the distribution of propaganda leaflets offering rewards for information and accusing SWAPO of atrocities. Teams of troops trained as 'communicators' visit settlements to give lectures and show films or videos.

Many police, soldiers and bantustan officials belong to political or 'cultural' front organisations called Etango in the Ovambo bantustan and Ezuva in Kavango. These organisations promote apartheid and bantustan ideology by organising training courses, holding meetings and distributing propaganda for this purpose.[17]

Mrs Jacobina Amukuhu, 37, of Okapanda claimed that she was beaten by Koevoet constables who assumed bicycle tracks near her house were those of a SWAPO freedom fighter active in that region.

After she told them that the tracks were those of her children, three white Koevoet constables grabbed her and beat her all over the body with clubs. While the beating was happening, she was carrying her two-year-old child on her back. Later Koevoet removed the child from her back and dropped the baby violently on the ground.

Namibia Communications Centre, 20.7.87

In the war zones, civilian personnel have been withdrawn from many administrative, health and educational tasks and many facilities have been closed. Independent church-run schools and clinics throughout the war zones have been shut on the orders of the authorities, and staff deported, detained or subjected to harassment for their suspected support of SWAPO.

Troops have been extensively deployed in bantustan administrations, particularly as medical personnel and teachers. There has been strong resistance, with protest boycotts and demonstrations in schools.

Wilkia Tobias Mule, an 18-year old schoolgirl from Ombalantu Secondary School, accused Koevoet (Crowbar) of beating her seriously on 2 July. The girl, a member of the Evangelical Lutheran Church in Namibia (ELCIN), said that Koevoet constables arrived at her home and kicked her repeatedly on the throat until she was near unconsciousness. Miss Mule was then subjected to electric shocks for half an hour and when she passed out completely, the soldiers went into her house and 'destroyed everything'.

Namibia Communications Centre, 20.7.88

Refugees in northern Namibia

Troops were withdrawn from schools and health facilities in Ovambo in 1985, following protests from the bantustan administration itself. The SADF was accused of attempting to seize total control of the health services and of organising unauthorised extracurricular activities for school pupils.[18]

A woman was killed, while two others were seriously injured last Sunday night, following a brutal attack by members of the South African Security Forces on outpatients and visitors at the Ombalantu Hospital, in northern Namibia. One of the injured women, Mrs Veronica Aukongo, 29, of Omulukila was nine months pregnant, and sources at the Kamhaku Hospital, Ombalantu, confirmed that she was shot in the stomach, causing the death of her unborn baby.

The Namibian, 9.10.87

Some schools, clinics and churches have been sabotaged and destroyed by troops. The church printing press at Oniipa was destroyed twice by the army, and in early 1977 13 schools were sabotaged by troops. The closure of health and educational facilities has led to a marked deterioration in social conditions in the war zones (*see Chapter 4*).[19]

A schoolgirl of 14 years from Onahende in the Ombalantu area, related how she was repeatedly raped by a member of the Security Forces, while another held her head tightly to the ground, and a third held her legs open.

The Namibian, 28.8.87

In some remote areas, the army has completely replaced the civilian infrastructure. In the Western Caprivi thousands of people are dependent on soldiers employed in Battalions 32 and 201 which are active in destabilising Angola. 32 Battalion is composed mainly of Angolans

Police vehicle with corpses tied to it

Lutheran printing press sabotaged by South African troops

recruited by the SADF and has borne the brunt of the fighting in Angola, suffering extensive casualties. 201 Battalion consists of nearly a thousand men classified in apartheid terms as 'Bushmen'. In the Bushmanland bantustan the army has also become the main employer.[20]

Even outside the war zones the SADF exerts a pervasive influence. Recruiting and registration for military service takes place at schools. White male secondary students and some black students are involved in paramilitary cadet training, which is directly controlled by the SWATF. The army is also involved in teacher-training courses and runs youth clubs.[21]

However, these efforts to 'win hearts and minds' have not produced the results which the

SADF has been seeking. One of the principal reasons behind South Africa's refusal to allow internationally supervised elections leading to independence for Namibia is its belief that SWAPO would win a free election. Support for SWAPO, as reflected in the resurgence of open political mobilisation during 1986 and 1987, has grown rather than decreased.

The terror perpetrated by the occupation forces has negated their attempts to win support, while the destruction of facilities and the economic collapse associated with the war have further alienated the Namibian people from the South African regime. Above all, the SADF cannot satisfy the basic demand of the Namibian people to determine their own future free from apartheid and colonialism.

ATTACKS ON NEIGHBOURING STATES

Unable to destroy SWAPO inside Namibia, the South African regime has increasingly resorted to attacking liberation-movement facilities in neighbouring countries. In particular, Namibian refugee settlements and transit centres such as the one at Kassinga have been targeted.

South African aggression against neighbouring states has gone far beyond attacks on refugees or the liberation movement. Pretoria has carried out a systematic campaign of military and economic destabilisation against the countries of Southern Africa. Following the independence of Angola and Mozambique after the collapse of Portuguese colonialism in the mid-1970s and the independence of Zimbabwe in 1980, the regime has attempted to establish itself as a 'regional power' and to dominate the region through political, economic and military pressure.

South African tank on manoeuvres

All the countries of Southern Africa have been attacked, directly or indirectly. South African assassins and commando squads have attacked representatives of SWAPO and the ANC and carried out economic sabotage. Mozambique has been devastated by the South African-backed Mozambique National Resistance (MNR or Renamo), and Angola has been repeatedly invaded by the SADF.

Angolan oil refinery sabotaged by South African commandos

The occupation of Namibia is crucial to Pretoria's war against independent Africa, as it provides direct access for South African troops to Angola and Zambia. Zimbabwe and Botswana also border Namibia as well as South Africa.

More than a million people have been displaced and over 100,000 have died as a result of South African aggression. The destruction of crops and transport networks has led to mass starvation and disease. The economic damage to the nine countries in the Southern African Development Co-ordination Conference (SADCC) in the 1980-84 period has been calculated at more than US£ 10 billion – the human cost is incalculable.[22]

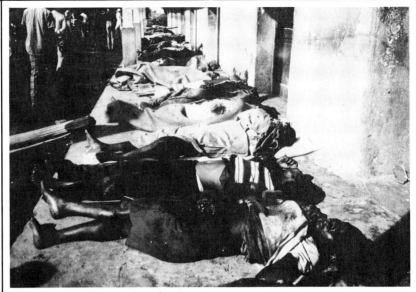

Victims of South African attacks on Angola

Angola

Angola, which freed itself from Portuguese colonialism in 1975 under the MPLA (Popular Movement for the Liberation of Angola), has borne the brunt of South African military aggression.

During 1975 South African troops invaded Angola in an attempt to prevent the MPLA from taking power and to install the UNITA movement, which assisted the invasion. Stopped just outside the capital Luanda by MPLA troops with assistance from Cubans to whom the MPLA had appealed for aid, the South African/UNITA force withdrew to northern Namibia.

A network of logistics facilities was established in the Kavango and Western Caprivi areas of northern Namibia to supply UNITA, and Angolan mercenaries were recruited into a new unit, 32 Battalion, based in the Western Caprivi. These forces, aided by regular South African troops and foreign mercenaries, immediately began destabilisation operations in Angola, destroying crops, livestock, settlements, villages and transport facilities.[23]

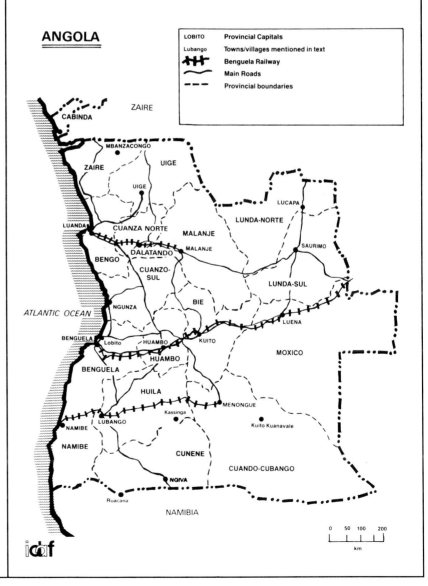

UNITA

UNITA, the National Union for the Total Independence of Angola, was formed in 1966 as a breakaway faction from organisations fighting Portuguese colonialism in Angola. By 1972, under the leadership of Jonas Savimbi, it had formed a working relationship with the Portuguese secret police. In return for help in fighting the main liberation movement, the People's Movement for the Liberation of Angola (MPLA), the Portuguese turned a blind eye to UNITA activities.

With the collapse of Portuguese authority in Angola in 1975, UNITA began to establish links with Pretoria. On 21 August that year UNITA formally declared war against the MPLA, and a South African armoured-car column invaded Angola from Namibian bases, attacking MPLA positions.

A joint South African-UNITA force advanced as far as the outskirts of the Angolan capital, Luanda, but was prevented from capturing it by the MPLA, which had by then called in Cuban assistance. The MPLA became the government of Angola on 11 November that year, and has subsequently been recognised as such by virtually all countries except the United States.

Remnants of UNITA withdrew with the South African forces to northern Namibia, where new bases were established. Other UNITA groups remained cut off in Angola and turned to banditry. Resuscitated by the South African Defence Force, UNITA soon began to play a vital role in Pretoria's destabilisation campaign against the MPLA government. UNITA groups working alongside South African units were infiltrated deep into Angola on missions of sabotage and destruction, and a UNITA presence was established in the south-east of Angola, in the remote and underpopulated Kuando Kubango province.

From Kuando Kubango, UNITA groups have fanned deep into Angola, especially the less densely populated eastern areas. They attack transport networks, agricultural and industrial enterprises, and terrorise villages. UNITA has been responsible for many atrocities, massacres and kidnappings.

The organisation is supplied from the militarised Caprivi Strip in north-eastern Namibia, through a network of South African military and civilian facilities. The South African 32 Battalion works closely with UNITA in operations in Angola, and other units are also deployed alongside UNITA.

South African Minister of Foreign Affairs with UNITA leader Savimbi, Cape Town, 1984

Effects of South African bombing in Angola

By the end of the 1970s, Angola was under persistent attack from UNITA and South African units. The South African Air Force was carrying out bombing attacks on villages, towns and industrial centres far to the north, and small sabotage squads were being infiltrated into the country. The Kassinga massacre in May 1978 marked a fresh escalation of aggression. (*See Chapter 6*).

Attacks increased substantially in 1981, partly because the new Reagan administration in the USA shared Pretoria's objective of undermining the MPLA government and indicated its support for South African aggression.[24]

A large invasion code-named 'Operation Protea' was carried out by up to 10,000 SADF troops in August 1981. This led to the capture of most of the key towns in Cunene province, from which 160,000 civilians were displaced. South African troops remained in occupation of Cunene, laying waste to the province. To the east, UNITA occupied most of sparsely populated Kuando Kubango province, and launched forays further north. UNITA bands were also active in the central highlands around the city of Huambo.[25]

During the following three years major battles took place as the apartheid forces attempted to extend their control northwards, especially during the mid-year dry seasons when the SADF could most effectively deploy its armoured and mechanised units. Many South African bombing and sabotage attacks were carried out against towns and installations vital to the Angolan economy.

At the end of 1983 South African troops were defeated in a series of battles in northern Cunene, while Angolan government forces largely drove UNITA out of the central highlands.[26]

International negotiations led to a South African agreement in February 1984 to withdraw from Angola and implement UN Resolution 435 for Namibian Independence (*see Chapter 2*). A South African-Angolan Joint Monitoring Group was established to supervise a ceasefire in Cunene province, but Pretoria failed to honour the agreement.[27]

In mid-1985 South African troops again mounted large-scale attacks on Angolan positions, mainly to prevent the defeat of its UNITA protege, which was being driven back towards its main base at Jamba by an Angolan offensive. The US administration also assisted UNITA by providing sophisticated arma-

South African tank captured by Angolan troops, Cuito Cuanavale, 1988

ments, which were reported to include Stinger anti-aircraft missiles.

SADF operations were stepped up again during 1986 and 1987, when thousands of South African troops were involved in fighting deep into Angolan territory.

In August 1987 the largest operation since 1981 was launched when the SADF moved into Kuando Kubango province to protect UNITA, laying siege to the town of Cuito Cuanavale early in 1988. By that stage, however, the Angolan ground and air defences had been considerably upgraded and the SADF's ability to inflict damage without itself suffering heavy casualties was restricted.[28]

After negotiations *(see Chapter 8)*, South African forces were forced to withdraw across the Namibian border in August 1988, leaving the Angolans in a far stronger military position than before.

Zambia and Botswana

From their bases in the highly militarised Caprivi Strip in Northern Namibia, South African troops have carried out repeated attacks on Zambia and Botswana.

About 600 South African troops based in the Caprivi Strip invaded Zambia in 1979 – at the time Zambia was being attacked by the minority-ruled Rhodesian regime, which was supported by Pretoria. The following year two SADF battalions equipped with armoured cars burnt villages and mined roads, apparently in an attempt to depopulate south-western Zambia. By 1981 famine and disease had become widespread in the area under attack.[29]

During this period groups of Zambian nationals trained in destabilisation techniques at Namibian army bases were infiltrated into Zambia to carry out banditry and sabotage. Later, UNITA became active along the Angolan/Zambian border, kidnapping and killing local people.[30]

Most South African aggression against Zambia involved the use of agents and saboteurs for attacks on economic targets and attempts at killing SWAPO and ANC leaders.[31]

A new type of operation took place in May 1986 when the South African Air Force bombed a refugee settlement near the capital Lusaka, killing one Namibian refugee and destroying buildings. The following year a South African commando raid was launched against the town of Livingstone, where a house once used by ANC officials was destroyed. There was a general escalation of activity against Zambia in 1987, and a number of South African agents were detained by the Zambian authorities.[32]

Botswana has been subjected to similar aggression. Bomb attacks, sabotage operations, aerial raids and border incursions have been carried out in efforts to pressurise the Botswana Government into political acquiescence. Some border violations, especially by troops based in the Caprivi Strip, appear to have been the result of indiscipline, but the majority are clearly calculated acts of aggression.[33]

Refugees have been kidnapped and assassinated, and 12 people were killed in a helicopter raid on the capital Gaborone in June 1985, launched from South African soil. Further commando-style raids took place during 1986 and 1987.[34]

Although the South African regime has caused considerable damage to neighbouring states through destabilisation and military aggression it has not regained the regional dominance it had before the mid-1970s. Through SADCC and the Front-Line States organisation, independent countries of Southern Africa have united against apartheid and continued their support for the liberation process in South Africa and Namibia.

In particular, the South African regime has failed to end Angolan support for Namibian independence, despite repeated invasions and attacks. SADCC, the Front-Line States and independent Africa as a whole, through the Organisation of African Unity, have continued to campaign for Namibian independence under UN Security Council Resolution 435.

8 LIBERATION STRUGGLE

For more than a century Namibians have struggled for their independence through diplomatic, political and military means.

An overriding feature of the liberation movement has been the drive to unite all Namibians for the independence struggle. The development of a national consciousness resulted in the formation in 1960 of the national liberation movement, the South West Africa People's Organisation (SWAPO), and the SWAPO slogan 'One Namibia, one Nation' has rallied Namibians to unity.

SWAPO was founded by migrant workers but it has mobilised all sectors of Namibian society. The movement has been recognised by the UN General Assembly as 'the sole and authentic representative of the Namibian people' until they can elect their own government in an independent country.

Initially SWAPO concentrated on diplomatic pressure and political mobilisation, but an armed struggle was launched in 1966 in the face of South African repression. From the mid-1970s this became the dominant form of the struggle, although diplomatic pressure, political mobilisation and civil disobedience campaigns continued. In the late 1970s, and again from the mid-1980s, SWAPO organisation of workers, youth and students was crucial to advancing mass political participation.

The Namibian churches have also played a vital role in popular mobilisation, taking an increasingly strong stand against the South African occupation.

RESISTANCE UNTIL 1960

After the defeat of Chief Mandume of the Kwanyama (1917), the Bondelswarts (1922) and the Rehobothers (1925), open military resistance was abandoned (*see Chapter 1*). However, Namibians in the centre and south of the country continued to resist South African colonialism by refusing to move into 'reserves' and by undermining South African stock-control and grazing regulations.

Migrant workers began to organise and there were strikes at the mines and at fish-processing plants. A branch of the South African Food and Canning Workers Union was set up in the fishing port of Luderitz during the 1920s. The Universal Negro Improvement Association (UNIA) led by Marcus Garvey was also active in Luderitz at this time.[1]

Thousands of Namibians joined the allied forces during the Second World War, in order to contribute to the fight for human dignity and freedom, but after demobilisation they were

SWAPO rally, Katutura

subjected to the same discrimination as other black Namibians and received scant reward for their services. Some of these men, such as Toivo ja Toivo, were later prominent in the national liberation movement.

To resist South African attempts to incorporate Namibia, particularly after the Nationalist party came to power in South Africa in 1948, Namibians began to petition the UN (see *Diplomatic Struggles below*). Many of these petitions were preceded by consultations with traditional councils and local people.[2]

New organisations

Although traditional leaders such as David Witbooi, son of Hendrik Witbooi, and Hosea Kutako played an important part in linking new struggles with earlier resistance, the initiative increasingly passed to modern political or educational associations, the churches and organisations representing workers.

Christianity, brought by colonial mission societies, spread rapidly amongst Namibians during the first half of the twentieth century.

By the 1940s Namibian Christians were struggling for local autonomy. Mass defections and strong pressure led in the 1950s to the Rhenish Mission being transformed into the independent Evangelical Lutheran Church, while the other main mission organisation, the Finnish Mission Society, became what is now the Evangelical Lutheran Church in Namibia (ELCIN). Under Namibian leadership, the churches began to play an important part in the liberation struggle (see *Chapter 5*).[3]

During the 1940s the African Improvement Society, another Garveyist organisation similar to the earlier UNIA, set up branches in major towns. One of the important contributions this organisation made to the national liberation struggle was the provision of independent education through evening classes for adults.[4]

Namibians studying in South Africa during the 1940s and 1950s made links with South African organisations, especially the African National Congress (ANC). On their return to Namibia some of these students formed a political party, the South West African National Union (SWANU) in 1959.

> I came here . . . to study and to gain more experience in political activity. I have made good friends, particularly among members of the African National Congress. It is now time to return and carry on the struggle in my own country.
>
> *Toivo ja Toivo in Cape Town, December 1958*

With a base amongst the intelligentsia, SWANU presented an articulate case for Namibian independence and gained support in the early 1960s. However, it was unable to become a national movement and did not make the transition to armed struggle.[5]

Workers played the most significant part in forming the national liberation movement. Luderitz became a centre of trade union activity in the early 1950s, mainly by the South African Food and Canning Workers Union, but activity was violently suppressed by the police.

In 1957 a group of Namibian workers and students led by Toivo ja Toivo formed the Ovamboland People's Congress (OPC), which became the Ovamboland People's Organisation (OPO). OPC was formally constituted in Cape Town where ja Toivo and some 200 Namibians were working or studying. By 1959 OPO was firmly established in Namibia. The organisation's initial aim was to campaign against the contract-labour system of forced migration, and thousands of workers soon joined.

Although basically organisations representing migrant workers, most of whom came from the Ovambo bantustan in the north of Namibia, OPO and OPC had the wider question of national liberation on their agenda.[6]

In Windhoek, where a branch had been launched under the leadership of Sam Nujoma, OPO joined forces with SWANU to oppose plans to remove the town's black population to the new segregated township of Katutura (see *Chapter 1*). A boycott of municipal services was started, and women organised demonstrations in the streets.

On 10 December 1959 police opened fire without warning on a demonstration led by women, killing 13 Namibians. This event became known as the Windhoek massacre and is now marked as Namibian Women's Day. The liberation movement was injected with a new sense of urgency, while police repression was intensified, forcing the national leadership underground or into exile.

> In response to that peaceful demonstration, which was predominantly made up of women, the racist South African police opened fire on the crowd of demonstrators, killing 12 and injuring 52 others. Among the 12 people killed was an elderly woman by the name of Kakurukaze ('old lady') Mungunda. She was hit by a bullet in the chest; realising that she had been fatally wounded, Mama Mungunda decided to die a heroic death, fighting to the last minute of her life against colonial injustice. Thus she stumbled, despite profuse bleeding, towards a parked car belonging to the superintendent of the city and managed to set it ablaze with a box of matches. Shortly thereafter, she died . . .
>
> The Namibian people commemorate the Windhoek uprising in order to pay tribute to those martyrs who dared to resist colonial injustices. Furthermore, it is as a tribute to the bravery and heroism of Kakurukaze Mungunda, that SWAPO has designated 10 December Namibian Women's Day.
>
> *Extract from SWAPO publication* Namibian Women in the Struggle

Sam Nujoma, addressing workers:

'We in OPO want to abolish this whole system and we want Walvis Bay to join us, to set up a branch of OPO. With so many contract workers here, especially in the fishing industry; you should have a strong branch working for you. We must work together – you, me, all of us – to end our oppression!'

When he finished some of the comrades spoke up, generally expressing strong approval though a few had fears and doubts. 'We are encouraged to learn where OPO stands,' said one worker, 'I think most of us would join OPO right now.'

'Then elect a branch secretary,' Nujoma said, 'and we can get to work right away. We'll send membership cards from Windhoek and everybody can join up.'

Vinnia Helao Ndadi, describing OPO organising

On 19 April 1960 OPO was reconstituted as the South West Africa People's Organisation (SWAPO). Sam Nujoma, who had been banished to northern Namibia, was elected president.[7]

SWAPO

SWAPO set itself the task of uniting Namibians to achieve independence, a democratic government in which all could participate, and a society free from apartheid, discrimination and the migrant labour system.

SWAPO was distinguished from other political organisations by its strong support from Namibian workers, and the organising work it carried out amongst the peasantry in the northern bantustans. By the end of 1960 several SWAPO branches had been established in the industrial and mining centres of the south and central areas, and there was also a network of committees in the north.

The movement concentrated on non-violent political mobilisation, but the Windhoek massacre and the repressive, intransigent attitude of the South African regime left the SWAPO leadership with few illusions about the likelihood of peaceful independence.

At the 1961 SWAPO congress in Windhoek contingency plans were made for military struggle. In succeeding years hundreds of

President Sam Nujoma

SWAPO supporters secretly left the territory to set up external offices of the movement, to prepare for independence and to establish military training facilities.

By 1964 the first trained combatants had returned to the Caprivi area to set up rural bases.

There are some who will say that they are sympathetic with our aims, but that they condemn violence. I would answer that I am not by nature a man of violence and I believe that violence is a sign against God and my fellow men. SWAPO itself was a non-violent organisation, but the South African Government is not truly interested in whether opposition is violent or non-violent. It does not wish to hear any opposition to apartheid. Since 1964, SWAPO meetings have been banned. We have found ourselves voteless in our own country and deprived of the right to meet and state our own political opinions.

Is it surprising that in such times my countrymen have taken up arms? Violence is truly fearsome, but who would not defend his property and himself against a robber? And we believe that South Africa has robbed us of our country.

Andimba Toivo ja Toivo, court statement 1968

Combatants of the People's Liberation Army of Namibia

Two years later, after the failure of the International Court of Justice to rule against South Africa's occupation of Namibia, the exiled leadership of SWAPO issued a call to Namibians 'to rise in arms and bring about our own liberation'.[8]

The onset of armed struggle, although foreseen by SWAPO, had profound effects on the young movement. Many of its leaders were detained, tortured and imprisoned; others were driven into exile. Repression took its toll on the organisation throughout Namibia and police carried out savage reprisals against local people suspected of supporting guerrillas.

SWAPO was largely driven underground, although it was not banned. At the end of 1969 the movement regrouped at a conference at Tanga in Tanzania, attended by delegates from inside and outside Namibia. Various departments were reorganised, a Youth League and Women's Council were formed and an Elders' Council was established to link traditional leaders with the modern liberation struggle. The military wing was restructured and renamed the People's Liberation Army of Namibia (PLAN) in 1973.[9]

The guerrilla struggle escalated rapidly during the 1970s, as a result of the peasant uprising and youth protest which followed the general strike of 1971-2 (*see the next section*), and because the collapse of Portuguese colonialism in Angola in 1974-5 opened the whole of Namibia's northern border to PLAN.

South Africa responded with a campaign of military terror in the north, and thousands of Namibians fled into Angola, Botswana or Zambia to seek the protection of SWAPO or to join PLAN. Schools, health centres and agricultural projects were set up by SWAPO to cater for the needs of tens of thousands of refugees, and the movement had to take on many of the functions of a government-in-exile.

The SWAPO Women's Council played a particularly important role in the refugee centres through its literacy, health and training programmes.[10]

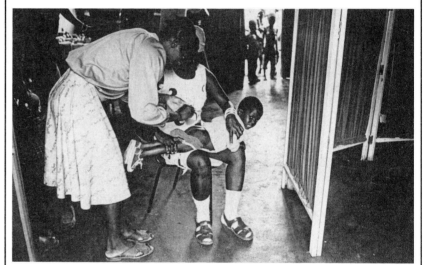

Health care, Kwanza Sul refugee centre, Angola

Literacy training, Kwanza Sul

SWAPO broadened its political support inside Namibia by forging alliances with other political groups, many of which disbanded to join SWAPO. Increasing support also came from within the churches, while the militant SWAPO Youth League gained a massive youth following. By the end of the decade the movement was a genuinely national one, representing a cross-section of Namibian society and all geographic areas.[11]

Namibian workers have played an important role in the national liberation struggle, and their organisation and actions during the 1970s and 1980s have

> It is impossible to divide workers' problems from the colonial oppression that we are experiencing in the country. You find that the colonial authorities make laws and most of these are regarding workers and the workers have no say in these laws because nobody in the country has any say. So what applies to the workers in particular, applies to the Namibian people in general.
>
> *Ben Ulenga, General Secretary, Mineworkers Union of Namibia*

transformed the nature and intensity of the struggle. (*Worker organisation and trade unionism is discussed in Chapter 3.*)

SWAPO's vision of a future Namibia was spelt out at a 1976 congress at which the movement adopted a political programme and a new constitution. A commitment was made to unite the Namibian people to work towards 'a classless, non-exploitative society based on the ideals and principles of scientific socialism'. A non-aligned anti-imperialist foreign policy, a programme for the development of culture, education and health, and an outline for economic reconstruction were also drawn up.[12]

SWAPO emphasises its non-racial objectives, and welcomes white as well as black Namibians as members. One of its main tasks is 'to combat all manifestations and tendencies of tribalism, regionalism, ethnic orientation and racial discrimination'. It has endorsed a bill of rights to protect individual liberties and democratic processes in a free Namibia. The movement is also committed to ending sexual discrimination, stressing the need to free Namibian women from male domination as well as colonial oppression.[13]

> We have adopted equality of sexes and we are committed to ensure that this equality is fully exercised in our movement in the interest of promoting the unity of purpose and action towards the total liberation of our motherland. It is the collective responsibility of both men and women to eliminate male chauvinism as well as promoting equality of the sexes among the members of SWAPO.
>
> *Sam Nujoma, SWAPO President, March 1988*

Although the president and many SWAPO leaders are based in exile, other office-bearers form an internal leadership which has survived repeated detentions and restrictions.

The organisation is divided into regions, districts, branches and sections, and is headed by a Central Committee elected at congress. Much organising has had to be carried out secretly.[14]

ARMED STRUGGLE

The first clash between SWAPO combatants and South African forces took place on 26 August 1966 when the police attacked a guerrilla base at Omgulumbashe in the Ovambo bantustan. Later that year guerrillas sabotaged government installations and then began attacks on police patrols.

Combatants returning from training outside Namibia had to face long and dangerous journeys, and military activity was generally restricted to the rainy season when movement was safer and easier. In the first two years, many SWAPO leaders and combatants were detained, tried and imprisoned (*see Chapter 6*).[15]

The guerrilla struggle was initially of low intensity. From the outset, the armed struggle was perceived primarily in political rather than military terms.

Combatants were seen as 'armed political militants' who carried out political organising work as well as military operations and were integrated into the local population.[16]

The close relationship between political and military struggle was demonstrated in the events following the 1971-2 general strike, which opened a phase of more intensive and generalised armed struggle.

Striking contract workers returned to their homes in the northern bantustans, especially Ovambo, where they united with local people to resist police attacks and repression by bantustan officials who were then being given greater powers by the South African authorities. Throughout Namibia, there were political demonstrations and protests against the South African occupation and its bantustan system.

New recruits strengthened SWAPO's military force, and by 1973 the South African authorities were dispatching large numbers of conscript troops to try to contain the uprising.[17]

The Portuguese colonial collapse in Angola in 1974 created conditions in which SWAPO could transform the popular uprising of the early 1970s into a military offensive. The SADF had relied on Portuguese military control of southern Angola; when this collapsed South African troops invaded Angola (*see Chapter 7*).

Despite the SADF operations, PLAN combatants began large-scale operations in Kavango and Ovambo. Tens of thousands of South African troops occupied the northern Namibian bantustans, but PLAN retained the military initiative, mining patrol roads, laying ambushes and attacking military bases.[18]

It was, moreover, SWAPO policy to integrate the military and the political arms of the struggle in the war zone. In selection, training and the conduct of the armed struggle, the motto has been 'it is always politics which leads the gun'. SWAPO's freedom fighters have always been first and foremost armed political militants.

In the fighting zones, cadres returning from training abroad were integrated into the local population. Some were assigned to enter the political organisation, to penetrate areas beyond the front line, or to recruit and train local volunteers. Many lived indistinguishably from the local peasantry. The freedom fighters were largely dependent on local party cells and sympathisers to organise the provision of their everyday supplies. The people were also their eyes and ears, shielding them from the occupation forces and providing them with essential military intelligence. But this was a reciprocal relationship. Some freedom fighters were also assigned to provide civilian services which the regime did not provide adequately, in particular medical assistance and literacy teaching.

SWAPO on the role of its combatants

Some PLAN combatants are trained medical assistants

During 1976 the number of guerrilla attacks and 'contacts' reported by the SADF was more than three times the total for the previous ten years, and incidents reported by the SADF continued at over 400 a year for the following ten years. Recorded incidents reached a peak in 1980-81, but an increasing number of clashes were not officially reported.[19]

The focus of the war has been in Ovambo, by far the most populous area of Namibia, but it has spread to Kavango and the harsh Kaokoveld, especially during 1982 and 1983. PLAN sabotage actions have also been carried out in the south and central areas of Namibia and in Windhoek; there was an increase in such actions in the the 1985-8 period. In most years, groups of guerrillas have penetrated the commercial farming areas south of Ovambo, attacking militarised white farms and engaging police or military forces.

The struggle has taken the form associated with guerrilla

South African army camp destroyed by PLAN, 1978

warfare – small groups of fighters have sabotaged communications networks and government facilities, while larger groups have laid ambushes and attacked army and police bases, usually at night. PLAN combatants usually disperse over wide areas, although larger mobile groups were used during 1983.

Popular support

Vastly outnumbered by the South African occupation forces and unable to establish major bases inside Namibia, PLAN has been able to expand its campaign by using guerrilla tactics and through local support from people who supply food, information and shelter.

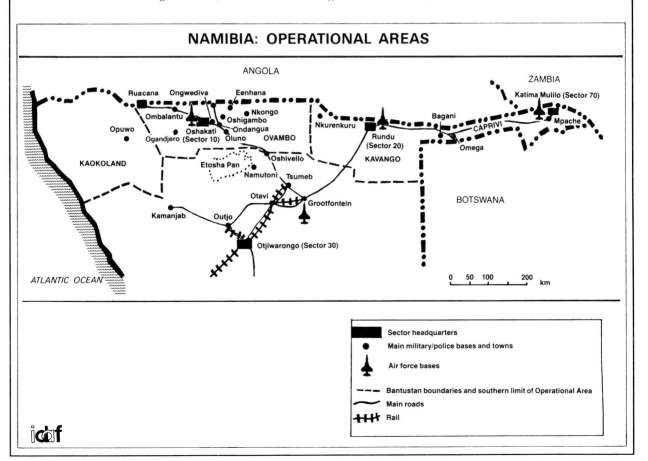

NAMIBIA: OPERATIONAL AREAS

ANGOLA
ZAMBIA

Ruacana Ongwediva Eenhana Katima Mulilo (Sector 70)
Ombalantu Nkongo Bagani Mpache
Opuwo Oshigambo Nkurenkuru CAPRIVI
Oshakati Ondangua
Ogandjero (Sector 10) Oluno OVAMBO Rundu Omega
(Sector 20)
KAOKOLAND Etosha Pan Oshivello KAVANGO
Namutoni
Tsumeb BOTSWANA
Otavi Grootfontein
Kamanjab Outjo
ATLANTIC OCEAN Otjiwarongo (Sector 30)

0 50 100 200 km

■ Sector headquarters

● Main military/police bases and towns

✈ Air force bases

--- Bantustan boundaries and southern limit of Operational Area

— Main roads

+++++ Rail

idaf

87

An assessment by South African military-intelligence officers in 1984 noted that SWAPO 'has an intensive intelligence gathering network whereby the public, especially the hundreds of cuca shops [trading stores] in Ovambo and Kavango, are involved and keep it informed as to the movement of the security forces'.[20]

Information on the fighting has been rigorously suppressed by the SADF, especially since 1983. Official information has consisted of little more than tallies of the number of PLAN fighters the 'security forces' claim to have killed. However, PLAN has regularly released detailed 'war communiques' documenting operations and reflecting far higher South African casualties than officially admitted.

The information black-out has enabled the South African regime to carry out a sustained propaganda campaign portraying the SADF as winning the war. Since 1980 the SADF has made annual claims to be on the brink of defeating PLAN. The SADF has said that its attacks on Angola, justified in terms of destroying SWAPO 'bases', have undermined PLAN's logistics. In fact, the occupation of southern Angola, which became a permanent feature of the war in 1980, failed to stop SWAPO military operations.

> The war in Namibia has become one of the debilitating factors that are propelling the inevitable collapse of the apartheid state. That war is costing South Africa more than one and a half million US dollars a day. It has resulted in the death of many South African soldiers and devastated the Namibian colonial economy. It has generated growing divisions, uncertainty and pessimism among the whites in Namibia. At the same time the heroism and martyrdom of PLAN combatants have captured the imagination of the Namibian people.
>
> *President Sam Nujoma, Press statement, London, 23.10.87*

PLAN has increasingly relied on support from within Namibia, and fighting units are permanently based inside the territory. During the 1980s PLAN activities have taken place throughout the year, not just during the rainy season, and SWAPO has annually reported an increase in the number of actions it has carried out.[21]

SWAPO's armed struggle forms part of the political campaign to pressurise South Africa into ending its presence in Namibia. The war increases the political and economic cost to South Africa of occupying Namibia. To the financial burden – estimated in the mid-1980s at more than R3 million a day – must be added the cost of the lives of hundreds of South African troops who have been killed and the resulting effects on white South African morale.[22]

PLAN has maintained its armed struggle for more than twenty years, forcing the South African regime to commit ever-increasing military resources to Namibia.

By 1986 Pretoria was claiming to have 'won the war' but SWAPO reported an increase in military activities in subsequent years, and several large sabotage operations and attacks on South African bases took place. Increasing support for the armed struggle was shown in 1986-8 when tens of thousands of Namibians attended SWAPO rallies in Windhoek and other towns, where cultural contributions concentrated on the role of PLAN.[23]

SWAPO rally, Katutura, 1986

BUILDING NATIONAL UNITY

During the 1970s, one of SWAPO's main concerns was to unite Namibians against the South African regime's bantustan plans, which had the aim of dividing the Namibian people and weakening their resistance, as well as undercutting international pressure for Namibian independence by dividing the country into a number of nominally 'independent' areas.

Workers, youths and students, the churches and some traditional leaders united with people living in the bantustans to oppose apartheid rule. SWAPO office-bearers were repeatedly removed from public activity by detention, torture, trial or banishment, but new leaders took their places.

Struggle against bantustans

In 1973 the South African regime prepared to foist 'self-governing' status on the Ovambo and Kavango bantustans, as part of its efforts to fragment Namibia and undercut UN demands for independence for the territory as a whole. SWAPO, especially its Youth League, led a boycott of the bantustan elections, organising both amongst contract workers in the south and in the bantustans themselves.

Despite the imposition of a state of emergency, mass detentions, the suppression of SWAPO meetings and the deployment of thousands of police and troops, the boycott was an overwhelming success in Ovambo. Afterwards, SWAPO leaders and supporters in the bantustan were rounded up and publicly flogged by the authorities, while Youth League members were detained, tried and imprisoned. Further detentions and trials of SWAPO leaders followed in 1974.[24]

Faced with strong international as well as Namibian opposition to the bantustan programme, the South African regime modified its strategy and from mid-1974 attempted to

SWAPO headquarters in the south, Gibeon

build opposition to SWAPO by establishing a pseudo-independent administration based on apartheid-defined 'population groups'. New bantustan elections were held in Ovambo after thousands of troop reinforcements had been sent there.

Bantustan leaders and representatives of political organisations participating in apartheid structures were selected to represent each of the 12 groups into which the Namibian population had been divided.

SWAPO organised rallies and united with other political organisations to oppose the South African scheme, which became known as the Turnhalle Conference. Most SWAPO meetings were banned, and there was another crackdown on the movement's leadership.

Support from the south

In May 1976 SWAPO organised a national conference at Walvis Bay, which reaffirmed the unity of the internal and external leadership and stated the principles on which the movement would negotiate with the South African regime.

SWAPO's drive to national unity was considerably strengthened in 1976-7 when several traditional leaders and political groups in the south and central areas of the country formally joined SWAPO. Amongst those who publically joined the liberation movement was Pastor Hen-

> SWAPO . . . has grown in the last few years to the genuine platform of all Namibian people organised by themselves in spite of all the attempts of the allies of the South African Government to disturb this development, in spite of all the persecution by the South Africans who forced many of its militants into death, captivity or exile . . .
>
> Today we have arrived at this crossroad and our choice is clear: We join unconditionally in the genuine nationalist platform of SWAPO created by our fellow-countrymen and not Turnhalle, the platform created by our enemy, the South African Government. We also ask seriously all other groups in a similar position to make the same step so that we – as a united and democratic power – can master this stormy period ahead of us.
>
> *Hendrik Witbooi (Gibeon), J. Stefanus (Vaalgras), S. Isaks (Keetmanshoop), H. Noeteb (Hoachanas), traditional leaders in southern Namibia, on joining SWAPO in 1976*

drik Witbooi, grandson of Hendrik Witbooi who had led the campaign against the Germans.[25]

The political mobilisation which had earlier taken place in the northern bantustans now occurred in the south and central areas. Students boycotted South African schools, workers were organised into the NUNW, and SWAPO's Youth League and Women's Council gained wide popular support.[26]

Struggle against the Democratic Turnhalle Alliance

Increased support for SWAPO inside Namibia was paralleled by growing international pressure, with the UN pressing strongly for Namibian independence (*see 'Diplomatic Struggle' below*). In a pre-emptive move in September 1977 Pretoria installed an Administrator-General in Windhoek to supervise a South African-controlled election. To lend some credibility to the exercise and to deflect international condemnation, some discriminatory laws, including the 'pass' laws, were removed.[27]

The Turnhalle Conference was dissolved, the participating groups forming the Democratic Turnhalle Alliance (DTA) for electoral purposes. SWAPO immediately began a campaign to resist the elections, which it saw as a South African attempt to keep the liberation movement from winning power in an internationally controlled independence process. The DTA received substantial funding and was backed by the army, police and most businesses. Pensions, jobs and other facilities were made dependent on DTA membership, and armed bands of DTA supporters were transported to different parts of the country to intimidate opponents.

SWAPO organised mass rallies in various centres, but many of these were banned or broken up by DTA supporters. Contract workers in Windhoek staged a one-day strike in protest at DTA violence. Leaders of SWAPO at national, regional and branch level were detained. The Lutheran, Anglican and Catholic churches issued a statement in May 1977 saying that torture had reached 'horrifying proportions'.[28]

By the end of 1978 the DTA had been installed in Windhoek as an administration. Various government departments were transferred to its authority in subsequent years.'Self-government' was introduced in July 1980. SWAPO, which had been

Arrest of demonstrator, 1978

brutally repressed in the intense conflict of 1977-8, continued its work in uniting opposition to the DTA. Although open organisation was no longer possible, the liberation movement was able to build popular resistance to the increasingly inefficient and corrupt DTA (*see Chapter 2*).

By 1982 it was clear that South Africa had failed to form the DTA into an alternative to SWAPO, and the administration was abolished the following year. Namibia was then ruled directly by Pretoria through the South African Administrator-General.

Struggle against Multi-Party Conference administration

The DTA was replaced in June 1985 by the Multi-Party Conference (MPC) administration, which was even less representative (*see Chapter 2*). Pretoria did not attempt to hold elections for the administration — an indication of the success of SWAPO in uniting Namibian opposition to the apartheid regime and its proteges.

Within two years the MPC was on the brink of collapse and there were signs that the South African regime was preparing to abandon it, aiming to resurrect the bantustan administrations instead. SWAPO retained the political initiative inside Nami-

bia, mobilising church, community and political organisations into the broad front of the Ai-Gams alliance to oppose the MPC and push for the implementation of UN Resolution 435 (*see Chapter 5*).

An 'independence' constitution drawn up by the bickering MPC factions was stillborn, and the administration failed in its efforts to establish the appearance of independence from South Africa. SWAPO moved on to the political offensive, stepping up its popular mobilisation, trade-union work and military attacks. Events such as May Day, Kassinga Day, and Namibia Day, which marks the anniversary of the launch of the armed struggle on 26 August 1966, were marked by large rallies and demonstrations around Namibia.

The detention and harassment of SWAPO leaders accompanied the banning or breaking up of meetings. Immanuel Shifidi, one of the founders of the movement and a recently released political prisoner, was killed by plain-clothes soldiers who attacked a SWAPO rally on 30 November 1986. However, such actions did not halt the resurgence of mass resistance. Throughout Namibia, people openly defied the authorities, while organisations representing workers, students, women and local communities grew in strength.[29]

DIPLOMATIC STRUGGLE

Since their early petitioning of the UN, Namibians have maintained pressure on South Africa through diplomatic activities and international campaigning. This struggle has been an integral part of SWAPO's strategy, but the liberation movement has never relied on external pressure alone.

Decisions by the UN General Assembly and Security Council in 1966 and 1969 – that South Africa had no right to occupy Namibia – were formalised in international law in 1971 when the International Court of Justice (ICJ) reached the same conclusion (*see Chapter 1*). South Africa refused to accept the ICJ ruling, but has been forced by subsequent UN pressure to follow what has been described as a 'two-track' policy.

While using delaying tactics to keep negotiations going with the UN, Pretoria has tried to build opposition to SWAPO inside the territory. It has sought to keep open possibilities of making the territory nominally independent under a compliant administration, while simultaneously seeking to weaken and modify UN plans for independence.

The apartheid regime has hoped that conditions would emerge where a government could be installed in Windhoek which would be both compliant with South Africa and internationally credible. Failing in this, it has continued its illegal occupation of the territory.[30]

Above all, Pretoria has been determined to prevent SWAPO coming to power through a genuine election brought about partly through an armed liberation struggle.[31]

Pretoria's plans to balkanise Namibia into bantustans led to increased pressure from the UN in the 1970s. In January 1976 the Security Council adopted Resolution 385. This demanded that South Africa end its bantustan programme, release all Namibian political prisoners, abolish discriminatory legislation, allow the return of Namibian exiles, withdraw its illegal administration from the territory, and allow the UN to supervise and control free elections in the territory. In December of that year the UN General Assembly recognised SWAPO as 'the sole and authentic representative of the Namibian people'.[32]

Contact Group

Two years previously the three permanent Western members of the Security Council – Britain, France and the USA – had used their powers of veto to prevent a mandatory arms embargo being imposed on Pretoria for its refusal to accept resolutions on Namibia. To forestall further UN demands for sanctions after South Africa's failure to meet the requirements of Resolution 385, the three powers established a 'contact group' to mediate between Pretoria and SWAPO. They were joined in this by the Federal Republic of Germany and Canada, which were then temporary members of the Council.[33]

By negotiating with the Contact Group, South Africa was freed from the immediate threat of international sanctions over Namibia.

Funeral of SWAPO leader Immanuel Shifidi, killed by South African soldiers in 1986

91

Walvis Bay

During the talks in 1977, South Africa moved to protect its long-term interests in Namibia by unilaterally annexing the deep-water port at Walvis Bay. The town and its surrounds were declared part of South Africa's Cape Province on the basis of their annexation nearly a century before by Britain. Later, Pretoria also claimed a number of small offshore islands.

Walvis Bay had been administered as part of Namibia since the League of Nations mandate and the UN rejected South Africa's claims to the territory. The General Assembly resolved that Walvis Bay was 'an integral part of Namibia' and that South Africa's action was illegal. The Security Council subsequently called for the 'reintegration' of Walvis Bay into the territory in Resolution 432 of July 1978.[34]

South African control of the enclave, which contains large military bases, would give Pretoria considerable economic and military leverage over any independent government in Namibia.[35]

Resolution 435

The Western contact group put forward new proposals for Namibian independence early in 1978, which made significant concessions to South Africa. The proposals undercut key provisions of the independence procedure set out in Security Council Resolution 385. Under the new plan, although the SADF would have to leave before a UN-monitored election to a Constituent Assembly was held, the South African administration and its police forces would remain in the territory until independence and Pretoria was not required to dismantle the bantustans.[36]

The South African government declared that it accepted the new proposals in principle. While SWAPO was considering its reaction, the South African regime intensified its repression of the liberation movement. On 4 May 1978 it attacked a major SWAPO refugee camp at Kassinga in Angola, massacring over 700 Namibians (*see Chapter 7*).

SWAPO was convinced that 'the strategic aim of [the] massacre was to force SWAPO to abandon the negotiations and thereby to bear the responsibility of the breakdown of the negotiations'.[37]

Prepared to make concessions to prevent further bloodshed, the SWAPO leadership accepted the modified proposals in July 1978. A UN representative was dispatched to Namibia and detailed recommendations for implementation were drawn up by the UN Secretary-General. These were approved by the Security Council on 29 September in Resolution 435.[38]

Security Council Resolution 435 specified a year-long independence process to be supervised by a specially established UN monitoring force known as the UN Transition Assistance Group (UNTAG). This would involve:

• A ceasefire, the partial demobilisation of South African forces and restriction to base of both SWAPO and South African military forces

• The repeal of all discriminatory and politically restrictive legislation, the release of political prisoners and the return of exiles and refugees

• National elections to a Constituent Assembly after a campaigning period

• The adoption of an independence constitution.[39]

It was clear even before Resolution 435 was adopted that South Africa, fearful of a SWAPO electoral victory, would baulk at its implementation.

Nine days before the adoption of the resolution, Pretoria declared that elections under the Turnhalle bantustan constitution would be held in Namibia. Defying UN condemnation, the regime went ahead with these illegal elections and later installed the DTA as a 'government' in Windhoek.[40]

The United Nations Security Council

Approves the report of the Secretary-General for the implementation of the proposal for a settlement of the Namibian situation and his explanatory statement,

Reiterates that its objective is the withdrawal of South Africa's illegal administration of Namibia and the transfer of power to the people of Namibia with the assistance of the United Nations in accordance with resolution 385 (1976),

Decides to establish under its authority a United Nations Transition Assistance Group (UNTAG) in accordance with the above-mentioned report of the Secretary-General for a period of up to 12 months in order to assist his Special Representative to carry out the mandate conferred upon him by paragraph 1 of Security Council Resolution 431 (1978), namely, to ensure the early independence of Namibia through free and fair elections under the supervision and control of the United Nations,

Welcomes SWAPO's preparedness to co-operate in the implementation of the Secretary-General's report, including its expressed readiness to sign and observe the cease fire provisions as manifested in the letter from the President of SWAPO dated 8 September 1978,

Calls on South Africa forthwith to co-operate with the Secretary-General in the implementation of this resolution,

Declares that all unilateral measures taken by the illegal administration in Namibia in relation to the electoral process, including unilateral registration of voters, or transfer of power, in contravention of Security Council Resolutions 385 (1976), 431 (1978) and this Resolution are null and void.

Extract from Resolution 435 of 29 September 1978

South African negotiators raised a series of new objections to the UN plan, revolving around the deployment of the various forces during the transition period. These issues were resolved at the end of 1979 by an agreement to establish a demilitarised zone along the Namibia-Angola border.

South African negotiators then raised objections to the 'partiality' of the UN towards SWAPO. However, as a result of further UN guarantees, by the end of 1980 the UN Secretary- General stated that there were only two outstanding issues to be resolved. These were Pretoria's 'lack of confidence' in the process, and the composition of the UN monitoring force, UNTAG. A pre-implementation meeting was convened in Geneva in January 1981 to prepare for independence.[41]

South African aggression

At Geneva, SWAPO President Sam Nujoma declared that he was ready to sign an immediate ceasefire. But the meeting soon broke up when the South African delegation again raised objections to the plan.[42]

The Western contact group blamed Pretoria for the breakdown of the talks. Despite this, the three permanent Western powers in the Security Council vetoed four resolutions providing for sanctions against South Africa.[43]

The triumph of the forces of liberation in Zimbabwe in the 1980 independence elections had jolted the apartheid regime out of any hopes that SWAPO would lose a UN-controlled election in Namibia. Internationally, the South African government was looking forward to closer links with the Western powers as a result of Ronald Reagan's accession to the US presidency. Pretoria correctly calculated that the new US administration would continue to protect it from sanctions even if it openly defied the world community.

The apartheid regime went on the offensive. In August 1981 thousands of South African troops invaded Angola, devastating areas near the Namibian border and occupying Cunene province. The USA cast a lone Security Council veto against a resolution condemning the invasion.[44]

Revising the Plan

General Malan, the South African Minister of Defence, made it clear to US negotiators that any settlement which would lead to a SWAPO government was unacceptable. Under US leadership, the contact group began revising the independence plan to meet South African objections.

Towards the end of 1981, new proposals were made, the chief of which was a set of constitu-

---

Malan flatly declared that the SAG [South African Government] can't accept prospects of a SWAPO victory which brings Soviet/Cuban forces to Walvis Bay. This would result from any election which left SWAPO in a dominant position. Therefore a SWAPO victory would be unacceptable in the context of a Westminster-type political system. Namibia needs a federal system. SAG does not rule out an internationally acceptable settlement, but could not live with a SWAPO victory that left SWAPO unchecked power . . .

SAG sees Savimbi in Angola as buffer for Namibia. SAG believes Savimbi wants southern Angola. Having supported him this far, it would damage SAG honour if Savimbi is harmed.

Second round of discussions went into greater detail on Namibia/Angola questions. Malan declared SAG view that Angola/Namibia situation is number one problem in Southern Africa. Angola is one place where US can roll back Soviet/Cuban presence in Africa. Need to get rid of Cubans, and support Unita. Unita is going from strength to strength, while SWAPO grows militarily weaker.

In his response Crocker agreed on relation of Angola to Namibia. USG believes it would be possible to improve US/South African relations if Namibia were no longer an issue.

Extract from US Administration record of conversation between South African Foreign Minister R.F. Botha and Defence Minister Magnus Malan, and US Assistant Secretary Chester Crocker, 15 April 1981

---

tional guidelines and a complex electoral system which would have made it difficult for SWAPO to achieve a two-thirds majority, now needed to approve the independence constitution. Although SWAPO was willing to accept the constitutional guidelines, the electoral proposals were abandoned when they proved unacceptable internationally. [45]

'Linkage'

In June 1982 a new element was formally introduced into the negotiations – 'linkage'. The Reagan Administration wished to obtain the removal from Angola of Cuban troops who had been brought into that country in 1975 to aid in repelling the South African invasion. The troops had been retained by Angola in the face of continuing attacks by South African forces based in Namibia and by the South African-backed UNITA force.

The US stated that the Cuban troops should be withdrawn in parallel with, or as a precondition for, a South African withdrawal from Namibia. This 'linkage' was seized upon by the South Africans, who used it to stall the implementation of the UN plan for Namibian independence.[46]

The 'linkage' of Angolan and Namibian issues was rejected not only by Angola and SWAPO, but also by the Organisation of African Unity, the Non-Aligned Movement, the Commonwealth, the UN General Assembly and, with the US abstaining, the UN Security Council itself. Nevertheless the issue provided South Africa with an ideal delaying mechanism and led to the virtual collapse of the negotiating process.[47]

Pretoria's strategy regarding Namibia became increasingly tied up with its regional objectives. 'Linkage' suited South Africa's aims of bringing down the Angolan Government, or weakening it by forcing it to negotiate with UNITA.[48]

In 1982-3 South Africa adopted an aggressive regional posture, mounting almost continuous attacks on Angola in particular. UNITA, which was increasingly supported by the US, was deployed in greater strength. At the end of 1983 the apartheid regime attempted a further massive invasion of Angola, with the objective of securing a decisive military advantage for itself and UNITA. The offensive failed.[49]

Diplomatic leverage

South Africa's delaying tactics did not pay off inside Namibia. SWAPO continued to escalate its military activities, despite the occupation of southern Angola which South African generals claimed would be the 'death blow' to the guerrillas. Pretoria's problems were compounded when the DTA administration collapsed in 1983.[50]

Having failed in its military campaign to destroy SWAPO and the Angolan government, the South African regime turned its attention towards the possibility of gaining a diplomatic advantage over the liberation movement.

To re-establish the option of unilateral 'independence', Pretoria began to cultivate the Multi-Party Conference (MPC) grouping in Namibia, which involved a number of small political groups and remnants of the DTA.[51]

The South African regime also undertook to withdraw its troops from Angola. The Angolan Government, stating that the Cuban troops in its country would not be needed once South African forces had withdrawn from Namibia and support for UNITA had ended, agreed to a gradual withdrawal of Cuban troops after the implementation of the UN plan for Namibian independence.

We accept the bona fides of SWAPO in its stated commitment to an immediate cease fire and the implementation of the process agreed to in UN Security Council Resolution 435. We reject the Cuban linkage introduced by the USA and South Africa as a prerequisite for the implementation of UNSCR 435 . . .

We urge that the United Nations reassert its prerogative and resume its responsibility through the Security Council and the United Nations Council for Namibia. We call for the enforcement of its resolutions consequent on its withdrawal of the mandate to South Africa, and its denunciation of South Africa's continuing illegal occupation. Specifically on the eve of its tenth anniversary, we urge that UNSCR 435 be enforced by direct UN intervention for its implementation forthwith.

Extract from letter to the UN Security Council from the Council of Churches in Namibia, September 1987

Demonstration against visit by South African State President P W Botha to Windhoek

PLAN commander points out details of South African military vehicle captured at Okanghudi, northern Namibia, October 1987

However, talks held between SWAPO and the apartheid regime in Lusaka in May 1984 broke down. Pretoria failed to honour its agreement to pull its troops out of Angola and its military campaign was soon renewed.[52]

In June 1985, as the MPC was installed as a 'transitional government' in Windhoek, the UN Security Council met to discuss Namibia. It declared the MPC administration 'null and void', rejected 'linkage' and urged member states to adopt a number of limited voluntary sanctions against Pretoria. The UN Secretary-General continued negotiations with the South African Government and at the end of 1985 he declared that 'all outstanding issues relevant to the UN plan' had been resolved.[53]

Faced with a nation-wide uprising inside South Africa and growing international pressure as a result of its domestic oppression and regional aggression, Pretoria adopted a defiant atti-

tude. It continued its efforts to promote the MPC administration in order to undercut the UN plan and carried out renewed attacks on Angola.[54]

During 1986 and 1987 a South African offensive was launched against SWAPO and the Angolan Government. This took the form of intensified repression inside Namibia, an international propaganda campaign to 'deglamourise' SWAPO by spreading false information about the movement, and a massive South African invasion of Angola during the second half of 1987. However, the invasion was repelled and the Angolans regained control of much of the territory occupied by South African forces in the early 1980s.

Although the MPC administration formulated a constitution for 'independence' under South African control, it was progressively weakened by internal disagreements and its draft constitution was rejected by Pretoria. In April 1988 the adminis-

tration was stripped of some of its powers and Pretoria again reasserted more direct control through the Administrator-General.[55]

Renewed pressure came from the UN in the form of Resolution 601 in November 1987. This reaffirmed the direct responsibility of the UN for Namibia and stated that 'all outstanding issues relevant to the implementation' of the UN plan had been resolved.[56]

South African military defeats in Angola at the end of 1987, coupled with international pressures, led to a series of talks during 1988 between the Angolan and South African Governments, with US and Cuban participation. Under discussion was a process in which the withdrawal of Cuban forces from Angola would follow the implementation of Resolution 435 and the end of South African aggression.[57] Agreement on these principles was reached in November 1988.

THE STRUGGLE IN THE 1980s

The 1980s have been marked by intensified military and political struggle by SWAPO in the face of South Africa's refusal to implement UN Resolution 435. Pretoria has dragged out negotiations with the UN while promoting internal alternatives to SWAPO in the form of the DTA and MPC. Intense repression has been directed against SWAPO but the liberation movement has steadily increased its support and by 1986 was able to operate openly inside Namibia.

The Namibian economy went into deep recession at the end of the 1970s. This, coupled with the war and a six-year drought, exacerbated unemployment and deprivation. However, in a largely unsuccessful attempt to establish a section of the population loyal to the DTA or MPC administrations, substantial wage increases were given to government officials and some state employees.[58]

Officials in the second-tier administrations enriched themselves through corruption, while the multiplicity of incompetent administrative bodies led to further declines in health, social and educational facilities.

South Africa's military occupation intensified and became increasingly brutal. The recruitment and conscription of Namibians into the occupation armed forces increased markedly, so that over 20,000 men were involved by 1988. Special mobile units such as Koevoet took over an increasing responsibility for the fighting against PLAN and were even more ruthless than regular troops, torturing and beating civilians.

With tacit approval from the Reagan Administration, from 1980 the South African regime concentrated on destabilising neighbouring states, particularly Angola. In 1982 southern Angola was invaded by South African troops and this occupation was maintained with only a partial break in 1985.[59]

SWAPO rally, Omaruru, northern Namibia, 1987

The largest ever invasion of Angola took place in the second half of 1987, but by May 1988 Angolan forces, with assistance from Cuban and SWAPO troops, had driven the invading army back to near the Namibian border. The South African forces were forced to withdraw totally in August 1988 after these military reverses, and a ceasefire was implemented.

While atrocities against civilians mounted inside Namibia, the occupation forces also stepped up their campaign to 'win the hearts and minds' of Namibians, in particular through military-backed organisations.[60]

Protected by US and British vetoes against sanctions in the UN Security Council, Pretoria was able to stave off international pressures to implement UN Resolution 435. However, the pressures for sanctions against South Africa mounted, especially after the 1984 uprisings began in South Africa and the regime responded by imposing successive States of Emergency.

In another development, the UN Council for Namibia sought to enforce Decree No. 1, for the protection of Namibia's natural resources, by taking legal action in the Netherlands against the

URENCO consortium which processes Namibian uranium in Europe.[61]

Pretoria was unsuccessful in its attempts to build an alternative to SWAPO inside Namibia, and the liberation movement consolidated its position as the representative of the vast majority of Namibian people.

SWAPO's increased strength inside Namibia and the growing momentum of the independence struggle were manifested in the mushrooming of student, worker and community organisations and the increasing outspokenness of the Namibian churches.

The Namibian National Students Organisation (NANSO), which was formed in 1984, played a prominent role in a wave of student protests in Namibia in the following years. NANSO rapidly organised branches in many secondary schools, as well as at the tertiary Academy in Windhoek, and articulated at annual conferences its programme of 'education for liberation'. Tens of thousands of students were involved in school boycotts during 1988. NANSO'S campaigns against apartheid education were paralleled by the establishment, mainly by churches, of schools outside the official education system, using alternative syllabuses.[62]

The churches themselves have become far more outspoken in their condemnation of the South African occupation and the campaign of terror by its armed forces. They were actively drawn into independence campaigning through the Ai-Gams alliance launched in 1986.

Workers organised into the new industry-based unions affiliated to the National Union of Namibian Workers carried out a number of large strikes in 1986-8, to which the authorities responded by raiding hostels and detaining union organisers. A strike by 4,000 mine workers at the Tsumeb Corporation (TCL) in July and August 1987 was one of the longest and most bitterly fought in Namibian history and in June 1988 up to 50,000 workers took part in a two-day strike in support of students boycotting classes, and in protest at police and army repression.[63]

Women's organisations have become increasingly active in campaigning against the oppression of Namibian women, following the lead of the SWAPO Women's Council. Community organisations including literacy groups, housing action groups, handicraft workshops, cultural and sports organisations and media collectives spread throughout Namibia during the 1980s. By 1987 one estimate was that there were 150 community organisations.[64]

Above all, it has been the growth in support for SWAPO, the movement's increasing organisational ability both inside Namibia and abroad, and the escalation of armed struggle over more than twenty years that has posed the biggest challenge to apartheid domination over Namibia. The struggle of the Namibian people has in turn been a catalyst for action by the international community.

CHRONOLOGY FROM 1800

1800
1878 Britain annexes Walvis Bay
1884 Namibia declared a protectorate by Imperial Germany

1900
June 1919 Treaty of Versailles: Germany forced to give up its colonies
December 1920 South Africa granted mandate over South West Africa on behalf of the British Crown
October 1922 Walvis Bay transferred to South West Africa administration
1946 UN General Assembly rejects South African proposal to incorporate Namibia – Pretoria refuses trusteeship

1950
July 1950 International Court of Justice (ICJ) rules that the mandate for South West Africa can be supervised by UN

1960
November 1960 Ethiopia and Liberia institute proceedings against South Africa before the ICJ
July 1966 ICJ decides that Ethiopia and Liberia lack standing to obtain judgement
October 1966 UN General Assembly revokes South Africa's mandate
May 1967 UN Council for Namibia established
March 1969 UN Security Council recognises the termination of the mandate and calls on South Africa to withdraw

1970
January 1970 Security Council declares that all acts taken by South Africa on behalf of or regarding Namibia are illegal
June 1971 ICJ advises that South Africa has an obligation to withdraw from Namibia and that states should recognise illegality of the South African occupation
October 1971 Security Council accepts the ICJ opinion
1972–3 Security Council negotiations with Pretoria yield no result and are terminated in December 1973
December 1973 General Assembly recognises SWAPO as 'sole authentic' representative of the Namibian people; UN Commissioner for Namibia appointed
September 1974 Council for Namibia enacts Decree No. 1 for the Protection of the Natural Resources of Namibia
December 1974 Security Council demands South African withdrawal by May 1975
January 1976 Security Council lays down procedure for South African withdrawal, elections under UN supervision and control, and Namibian independence (Resolution 385)
April 1977 Western Contact Group begins discussions
September 1977 South Africa appoints Administrator-General with executive powers and proclaims Walvis Bay South African territory
September 1978 Contact Group proposals for Namibian independence approved by Security Council (Resolution 435)
1979-80 Pretoria raises successive objections to 435

1980
January 1981 Pre-Implementation Talks in Geneva: South Africa refuses to sign ceasefire
June 1982 President Reagan launches 'linkage' policy, demanding withdrawal of Cuban troops from Angola before Namibian independence
October 1983 Security Council rejects linking Namibian issue with 'extraneous issues'
December 1983 Security Council demands South African withdrawal from Angola and declares Angola is entitled to compensation
May 1984 Lusaka talks between South Africa and SWAPO break down because of South African insistence on 'linkage'
November 1984 Angolan government submits proposal for phased withdrawal of Cuban troops with implementation of Resolution 435
May 1985 Security Council declares establishment of Multi-Party Conference 'transitional government' null and void
November 1986 Security Council reaffirms its direct UN responsibility for Namibia and declares 'all outstanding issues' relevant to UN plan for independence have been resolved
May 1988 Talks begin between South Africa, Angola, US and Cuba resulting in July in agreement on principles for implementation of UN plan for independence
August 1988 Ceasefire in Angola; South Africa withdraws

1800

1858 Treaty of Hoachanas governing relations between leaders in the south and centre of Namibia
1860 Rehoboth republic established
1891-4 Nama resist German colonisation
1894 Large-scale migrant labour begins

1900

1904-5 Herero and Nama uprising against Germans; German genocide policy from October 1904
September 1907 Guerilla leader Jacob Morenga killed
July 1915 Germans surrender to invading South Africans
February 1917 King Mandume of Oukwanyame killed
May 1922 South African massacre of Bondelswarts
April 1925 Rehoboth resistance crushed
1932 King Ipumbu of Uukwambi deposed by force

1950

1954-5 Mass demonstrations in north against contract labour system
1957 Ovamboland People's Congress formed in Cape Town
1958 Ovamboland People's Organisation launched in Namibia
May 1959 Formation of South West African National Union (SWANU)
December 1959 Windhoek Massacre

1960

April 1960 South West African People's Organisation (SWAPO) formed
May 1964 South African Odendaal Commission recommends bantustan programme
August 1966 SWAPO proclaims armed struggle; first engagement at Omgulumbashe
1968 Pretoria implements bantustan programme
December 1969 SWAPO Consultative Conference at Tanga in Tanzania

1970

June–August 1971 Nationwide demonstrations in support of ICJ ruling that South Africa's occupation is illegal
December 1971 National strike by 20,000 contract workers
February 1972 Peasant uprising in north leads to State of Emergency
June 1974 Portuguese colonialism in Angola collapses; thousands of Namibians leave as volunteers for armed struggle
August 1975 South African troops invade Angola
September 1975 South Africa sets up Turnhalle constitutional conference
November 1976 Widespread school boycotts
May 1978 South African troops massacre 700 Namibians at Kassinga
December 1978 South Africa installs Democratic Turnhalle Alliance (DTA) administration in Windhoek
April 1979 Most of SWAPO leadership inside Namibia detained

1980

October 1980 South Africa introduces conscription for all Namibian males
August 1981 South African troops occupy areas of Southern Angola
January 1983 DTA administration dissolved; Pretoria resumes direct authority
1984 Formation of Namibian National Students Organisation (NANSO)
February 1984 South African troops fail to withdraw from Angola following ceasefire agreed with Angolan government
June 1985 South Africa installs Multi-Party Conference administration
April 1986 SWAPO, churches and other groups form Ai-Gams alliance to campaign for independence; mass rallies follow
July 1986 Supreme Court lifting of ban on SWAPO meetings is followed by large rallies throughout Namibia
September 1986 Namibian Food and Allied Workers Union (NAFAU) launched
November 1986 Mineworkers Union of Namibia (MUN) launched
1987 Nationwide worker organisation; strikes, formation of new unions, police attacks and raids on workers' residences; SWAPO rallies throughout Namibia
July–August 1987 Miners strike at Tsumeb
August 1987 South African invasion of Angola leads to strategic defeat at end of year
March 1988 Pupils begin nationwide school boycotts, demanding removal of army bases
April 1988 Pretoria assumes new powers over MPC administration
June 1988 Workers stage national two-day stay-away in support of student boycotts

NAMIBIA: COMMEMORATIVE DATES

19 April	Founding of SWAPO (1960)
4 May	Kassinga Day (massacre of refugees in Angola, 1978)
18 May	Heroes Day (death of SWAPO military commander Tobias Hainyeko, 1967)
26 August	Namibia Day (launch of armed struggle, 1966)
27 October	Namibia Week (UN and international solidarity activities around date when UN General Assembly revoked South Africa's mandate, 1966)
10 December	Namibia Women's Day (Windhoek Massacre, 1959)

Abbreviations

ANC	African National Congress
CCN	Council of Churches in Namibia
CDM	Consolidated Diamond Mines
COIN	(Koevoet Police) Counter-Insurgency Unit
DTA	Democratic Turnhalle Alliance
ELC	Evangelical Lutheran Church
ICJ	International Court of Justice
ICU	Industrial and Commercial Workers Union
MANWU	Metal and Allied Namibian Workers Union
MNR	Mozambique National Resistance
MPC	Multi-Party Conference
MPLA	Popular Movement for the Liberation of Angola
MUN	Mineworkers Union of Namibia
NAFAU	Namibian Food and Allied Workers Union
NAMPA	Namibian Press Agency
NANSO	Namibia National Students Organisation
NAPWU	Namibian Public Workers Union
NATAU	Namibia Transport and Allied Workers Union
NPU	Newspaper Union (of South Africa)
NTU	Namibia Trade Union
NUNW	National Union of Namibian Workers
OPC	Ovamboland People's Congress
OPO	Ovamboland People's Organisation
PLAN	People's Liberation Army of Namibia
RTZ	Rio-Tinto Zinc
SADCC	Southern African Development Co-ordination Conference
SADF	South African Defence Force
SWABC	South West African Broadcasting Corporation
SWACOL	South West African Confederation of Labour
SWANLA	South West African Native Labour Association
SWANU	South West African National Union
SWAPO	South West African People's Organisation
SWAPOL	South West African Police
SWATF	South West Africa Territory Force
TCL	Tsumeb Corporation
TGNU	Transitional Government of National Unity
UNCN	United Nations Council for Namibia
UNIA	Universal Negro Improvement Association
UNIN	United Nations Institute for Namibia
UNITA	National Union for the Total Independence of Angola
UNTAG	United Nations Transition Assistance Group

LIST OF MAPS, GRAPHS, CHARTS AND TABLES

MAPS

GRAPHS, CHARTS AND TABLES

BIBLIOGRAPHY

Newspapers, periodicals and serials

Action on Namibia, Namibia Support Committee, London.
Africa Insight, Africa Institute of South Africa, Pretoria.
Africa Institute Bulletin, Africa Institute of South Africa, Pretoria.
Cape Times, Cape Town.
CCN Information, Council of Churches in Namibia, Windhoek.
Combatant, People's Liberation Army of Namibia.
Daily Dispatch, East London
Financial Mail, Johannesburg.
Financial Times, London.
Focus on Political Repression in Southern Africa, IDAF, London.
Geoforum, Oxford.
Government Gazette, Windhoek.
IDAF Briefing Papers, IDAF, London.
IDOC Bulletin, International Documentation Committee, Rome.
Journal of Modern African Studies, Cambridge.
Journal of Southern African Affairs, Washington.
Journal of Southern African Studies, Oxford.
Namibia Digest, Windhoek.
Namibian Review, Windhoek.
Namibian, Windhoek.
Review of African Political Economy, Sheffield.
SASPU National, South African Students Press Union, Johannesburg.
Soldier of Fortune, Boulder, Colorado.
South, Cape Town.
South African Labour Bulletin, Johannesburg.
Southern Africa Focus, Namibia Features and Press Agency, Windhoek.
Southscan, London.
Star, Johannesburg.
Sunday Star, Johannesburg.
Survey of Race Relations, Annual, Institute of Race Relations, Johannesburg
Windhoek Advertiser, Windhoek.
Windhoek Observer, Windhoek.

Books and articles

Abrahams, K., 1980, 'Representative authorities and ethnic elections', *Namibian Review*, July-August.
Abrahams, O., 1986, 'Education in Namibia today', *IDOC Bulletin*, No. 3.
Allison, C., 1986, *'It's Like Holding the Key to Your Own Jail': Women in Namibia*, World Council of Churches, Geneva.
Amnesty International, 1982, *Human Rights Violations in Namibia*, Amnesty International, London.
Andersson, N., & Marks, S., 1987, 'Work and health in Namibia: preliminary notes', *Journal of Southern African Studies*, Vol. 13, No. 2.
Angula, L. S., 1984, 'Theories fall apart: an exploration into the class position of the Namibian migrant labourer', *Namibia 1884-1984: 100 Years of Foreign Occupation, 100 Years of Struggle* Conference, London, September.
Anti-Apartheid Movement, 1986, 'The Namibian economy: key statistics', *Free Namibia! Mobilising Conference*, London, October.
Asmal, K., 1980, *The Status of Combatants of the Liberation Movement of South Africa under the Geneva Conventions of 1949 and Protocol I of 1977*, United Nations Centre Against Apartheid, New York (Notes and Documents 10-80).
Bley, H., 1967, 'German South West Africa', in R. Segal & R. First (eds), *South West Africa: Travesty of Trust*, André Deutsch, London.
Bradford, R.L., 1967, 'Blacks to the wall', in R. Segal & R. First (eds.), *South West Africa: Travesty of Trust*, André Deutsch, London.
British Council of Churches, 1987, *Namibia – A Nation Wronged*, British Council of Churches, London.
Bureau for Research, 1987, *Urbanisation in South-West Africa/Namibia: An Exploratory Study*, Academy, Windhoek.

Cawthra, G., 1986 *Brutal Force: The Apartheid War Machine*, IDAF, London.
CIIR, 1984, *South African Occupation and the Namibian Economy*, Catholic Institute for International Relations, London.
CIIR, 1986, *Namibia in the 1980s*, Catholic Institute for International Relations, London.
Cronje, G. & Cronje, S., 1979, *The Workers of Namibia*, IDAF, London.
Department of Governmental Affairs, 1987, *Namibia: The Economy*, Information Service, Department of Governmental Affairs, Windhoek.
Dugard, J., 1973, *The South West Africa/Namibia Dispute: Documents and Scholarly Writings on the Controversy between South Africa and the United Nations*, University of California Press, Berkeley.
Du Pisani, A., 1986, *SWA/Namibia: The Politics of Continuity and Change*, Jonathan Ball, Johannesburg.
Du Plessis, P. J., 1986, 'Profile of smaller urban areas in SWA/Namibia', in G. J. Merrington, *Some Aspects of Urbanisation and Its Management in SWA/Namibia*, Paper to the Development Seminar, Windhoek, November 1986.
Ellis, J., 1984, *Education, Repression and Liberation: Namibia*, Catholic Institute for International Relations/World University Service, London.
Emmett, T., 1986, 'Popular resistance in Namibia 1920-1925', in T. Lodge (ed.), *Resistance and Ideology in Settler Societies*, Ravan Press, Johannesburg.
First, R., 1963, *South West Africa*, Penguin, Harmondsworth.
Geldenhuys, D., 1984, *The Diplomacy of Isolation: South African Foreign Policy Making*, Macmillan, Johannesburg.
Gordon, R. J., 1978, 'Variations in migration rates: the Ovambo case', *Journal of*

Southern African Affairs, Vol. 3, No. 3.

Green, R., 1987, 'Namibia: dependence, destabilisation and development', Conference on Namibia, Oxfam, London, May.

Hanlon, J., 1986, Beggar Your Neighbours: Apartheid Power in Southern Africa, Catholic Institute for International Relations, London.

Holness, M., 1986, 'Angola: the struggle continues', in P. Johnson & D. Martin, Destructive Engagement: Southern Africa at War, Zimbabwe Publishing House, Harare.

Horrel, M., 1978, Laws Affecting Race Relations in South Africa, South African Institute of Race Relations, Johannesburg.

Hortors, 1987, Hortors Diary and Law List for Southern Africa, Hortors Stationery, Johannesburg.

IDAF, 1980, Namibia: The Facts, IDAF, London.

IDAF, 1981, Remember Kassinga, IDAF, London (Fact Paper on Southern Africa, No. 9).

IDAF, 1982, The Capture and Treatment of Guerilla Combatants and Other Prisoners-of-War by South African Forces Operating in Namibia, IDAF, London.

IDAF, 1985, A Nation in Peril: Health in Apartheid Namibia, IDAF, London (Fact Paper on Southern Africa, No. 13).

IDAF, 1987, Working under South African Occupation: Labour in Namibia, IDAF, London (Fact Paper on Southern Africa, No. 14).

Katjavivi, P. J., 1984, 'The development of anti-colonial forces in Namibia', Namibia 1884-1984: 100 Years of Foreign Occupation, 100 Years of Struggle, Conference, London, September.

Katjavivi, P.J., 1988, A History of Resistance in Namibia, James Currey, London.

Konig, B., 1983, Namibia: The Ravages of War, IDAF, London.

Landis, E., 1984, 'Namibia in the international context: the frustration of independence', Namibia 1884-1984: 100 Years of Foreign Occupation, 100 Years of Struggle, Conference, London, September.

Lindsay, J., 1987, 'The politics of population control in Namibia', Women, Colonialism and Commonwealth Seminar, Institute of Commonwealth Studies, University of London, April.

Lobstein, T., & NSC, 1984, Namibia: Reclaiming the People's Health, Action on Namibia Publications, Namibia Support Committee, London.

Melber, H., 1983, Our Namibia: A Social Studies Text Book, Terre des Hommes, Osnabrück.

Merrington, G. J., 1986, Some Aspects of Urbanisation and Its Management in SWA/Namibia, Paper to the Development Seminar, Windhoek, November.

Minty, A., 1986, 'Namibia: a review of developments since the 1980 International Conference in Solidarity with the People of Namibia', Second Brussels International Conference on Namibia, Brussels, May.

Moorsom, R., 1982, Transforming a Wasted Land, Catholic Institute for International Relations, London.

Moorsom, R., 1984, Walvis Bay: Namibia's Port, IDAF, London.

Murray-Hudson, A., 1983, 'SWAPO: solidarity with our sisters', Review of African Political Economy, No. 27/28.

O'Callaghan, M., 1977, Namibia: The Effects of Apartheid on Culture and Education, UNESCO, Paris.

O'Linn, B., 1987, 'UN Resolution 435 (1978) and the future of Namibia', in G. Totemeyer, V. Kandetu & W. Werner (eds.), Namibia in Perspective, Council of Churches of Namibia, Windhoek.

SACBC, 1982, Report on Namibia, Southern African Catholic Bishops Conference, Pretoria.

Simon, D., 1985, 'Decolonisation and local government in Namibia: the neo-apartheid plan, 1977-83', Journal of Modern African Studies, No. 23.

Simon, D., 1986, 'Desegregation in Namibia: the demise of urban apartheid?', Geoforum, No. 2.

Simon, D., 1988, 'Urban squatting, low-income housing, and politics in Namibia on the eve of independence', in R. A. Obudho & C. C. Mhlanga (eds.), Slum and Squatter Settlements in Sub-Saharan Africa, Praeger, New York.

Simon, D. & Moorsom, R., 1986, 'Namibia's political economy: a contemporary perspective', The Southern African Economy after Apartheid Conference, University of York Centre for Southern African Studies, 29 September to 2 October.

Simon, D. & Moorsom, R., 1987, 'Namibia's political economy: a contemporary perspective', in G. Totemeyer, V. Kandetu & W. Werner (eds), Namibia in Perspective, Council of Churches of Namibia, Windhoek.

Simons, H. J., 1967, 'Techniques of domination: South Africa's colonialism', in R. Segal & R. First (eds), South West Africa: Travesty of Trust, André Deutsch, London.

Smith, S., 1986, Namibia: A Violation of Trust, Oxfam, Oxford.

Soggot, D., 1986, Namibia: The Violent Heritage, Rex Collings, London.

South West Africa, Administrator-General, 1982, Die Verslag van die Kommissie van Ondersoek na Gesondheidsdienste in Suidwes-Afrika.

Strauss, A., 1987, 'Community organisation in Namibia', in G. Totemeyer, V. Kandetu & W. Werner (eds), Namibia in Perspective, Council of Churches of Namibia, Windhoek.

SWAPO, (n.d) Namibia: Culture and the Liberation Struggle,

SWAPO Department of Information and Publicity, Luanda.

SWAPO, 1976, *Political Program of the South West Africa People's Organisation*, SWAPO Central Committee, Lusaka.

SWAPO, 1978a, *Information on Namibian Political Prisoners*, SWAPO, Lusaka.

SWAPO, 1978b, *Information on SWAPO: An Historical Profile*, SWAPO Department of Information and Publicity, Lusaka.

SWAPO, 1978c, *Information on the People's Resistance 1976-1977*, SWAPO Department of Information and Publicity, Lusaka.

SWAPO, 1980, 'Namibia: towards genuine independence', *International Conference in Solidarity with the Struggle of the People of Namibia*, Paris, September.

SWAPO, 1981, *To be Born a Nation: The Liberation Struggle for Namibia*, Zed Press, London.

SWAPO, Women's Solidarity Campaign, 1984, 'Race, gender and class: theoretical perspectives and implications for building solidarity in Britain with Namibian women', *Namibia 1884-1984: 100 Years of Foreign Occupation, 100 Years of Struggle* Conference, London, September.

UN, 1983, *Namibia: A Unique UN Responsibility: Highlights of United Nations Action in Support of Freedom and Independence for Namibia*, United Nations, New York.

UNCN, 1983, 'Political developments related to Namibia', *International Conference in Support of the Namibian People for Independence*, Paris, April.

UNIN, 1984, *Health Sector Policy Options for Independent Namibia*, United Nations Institute for Namibia, Lusaka.

UNIN, 1986, *Namibia: Perspectives for National Reconstruction and Development*, United Nations Institute for Namibia, Lusaka.

UNIN, 1987, *Namibia: A Direct United Nations Responsibility*, United Nations Institute for Namibia, Lusaka.

Van der Merwe, J. H. (ed.), 1983, *National Atlas of South West Africa (Namibia)*, Institute of Cartographic Analysis, University of Stellenbosch/Directorate Development Co-ordination, Windhoek.

Von Garnier, C. (ed) 1986, *Katutura Revisited 1986*, Angelus Printing, Windhoek.

Werner, W., 1984, 'Struggles in the Namibian countryside 1915 to 1950: some preliminary notes', *Namibia 1884-1984: 100 Years of Foreign Occupation, 100 Years of Struggle* Conference, London, September.

Werner, W., 1987, 'Ethnicity and reformism in Namibia', in G. Totemeyer, V. Kandetu & W. Werner (eds), *Namibia in Perspective*, Council of Churches of Namibia, Windhoek.

Wolfers, M. & Bergerol, J., 1983, *Angola in the Frontline*, Zed Press, London.

Wood, B., 1987, 'The battle for trade unions in Namibia', *South African Labour Bulletin*, May/June.

WUS, 1987, *Namibia: Education in Conflict*, World University Service (UK) and British Defence and Aid Fund for Southern Africa, London.

Ya-Otto, J., 1982, *Battlefront Namibia*, Heinemann, London.

REFERENCES AND NOTES

CHAPTER 1: Historical Background

1 SWAPO, 1981, pp. 12-15
2 Soggot, 1986, p. 17
3 Bley, 1967, p. 45; Gordon, 1978, p. 263; Du Pisani, 1986, p. 33
4 Du Pisani, 1986, p. 33
5 Bley, 1967, p. 48
6 Soggot, 1986, p. 7
7 Bley, 1967, p. 50
8 Dugard, 1973, p. 72
9 Du Pisani, 1986, p. 56
10 First, 1963, p. 106; Soggot, 1986, p. 20; Du Pisani, 1986, p. 57
11 Bradford, 1967, p. 98
12 Du Pisani, 1986, p. 92; Soggot, 1986, p. 21
13 Bradford, 1967, p. 90; Gordon, 1978, p. 266
14 Du Pisani, 1986, p. 62
15 Soggot, 1986, p. 18
16 Bradford, 1967, pp. 89-92; Gordon, 1978, p. 267
17 First, 1963, p. 101; Bradford, 1967, pp. 92-3; Gordon, 1978, p. 269
18 Bradford, 1967, p. 92; Du Pisani, 1986, p. 58
19 First, 1963, p. 100
20 SWAPO, 1981, pp. 162-4
21 SWAPO, 1981, pp. 162-4; Emmett, 1986, pp. 20-35
22 Dugard, 1973, pp. 89-111
23 Dugard, 1973 pp. 112-9; Du Pisani, 1986, pp. 107-23
24 Dugard, 1973, pp. 236-9; SWAPO, 1981, pp. 135-6
25 First, 1963, pp. 192-5
26 SWAPO, 1981, pp. 172-5
27 Landis, 1984, p. 4; SWAPO, 1981, p. 168
28 Dugard, 1973, pp. 239-76
29 SWAPO, 1981, p. 177
30 Dugard, 1973, pp. 379-408; UNCN, 1983, p. 3
31 Dugard, 1973, pp. 409-13; UN, 1983 p. 7
32 UNCN, 1983, p. 4; UN, 1983, pp. 10-12

CHAPTER 2: The Apartheid Colony

1 Dugard, 1973, p. 267
2 First, pp. 142-50; UNIN, 1986, p 39
3 *Survey of Race Relations*, 1964, pp. 362-3
4 SWAPO, 1981, p. 61
5 *Survey of Race Relations*, 1970, p. 284, *Namibian*, 6.11.87
6 South West Africa, 1982 p. 90; *Africa Institute Bulletin*, No. 5, 1984, p. 56
7 Anti-Apartheid Movement, 1986; UNIN, 1988, pp. 66-73
8 South West Africa, 1982 p. 91; Anti-Apartheid Movement, 1986
9 Merrington, 1986, p. 13; Bureau for Research, 1987, p. 9
10 Van der Merwe, 1983
11 Simon, 1986, p. 293
12 Von Garnier, 1986
13 Simon, 1986, p. 289
14 *Sunday Star*, 29.3.87

15 Simon, 1986, p. 304; *Sunday Star*, 29.3.87
16 Horrel, 1978, pp. 484-7
17 *Focus*, No. 44, January-February 1983, pp. 1-2; Du Pisani, 1986, p 436; Geldenhuys, 1984, pp 91-6
18 *IDAF Briefing Paper*, No. 2, July 1981, pp. 1-3
19 *IDAF Briefing Paper*, No. 2, July 1981
20 *IDAF Briefing Paper*, No. 6, July 1982
21 *Focus*, No. 60, September-October 1985, pp. 10-11
22 *IDAF Briefing Paper*, No. 20, May 1986
23 *IDAF Briefing Paper*, No. 22, May 1988; No. 23, May 1988
24 Horrel, 1978, pp. 486-92
25 *Survey of Race Relations*, 1975, pp. 332-3; Horrel, 1978 pp. 495-7; SWAPO, 1981, p. 137
26 Kiljunen, 1983, pp. 97-8; Cawthra, 1986, pp. 199-200
27 *IDAF Briefing Paper*, No. 2, July 1981
28 Abrahams, 1980, pp. 4-12; *IDAF Briefing Paper*, No. 2, July 1981; Simon, 1985, pp. 509-11; UNIN, 1986, p. 52
29 Werner, 1987, p. 6
30 *Windhoek Advertiser*, 8.3.88
31 Simon, 1985, pp. 512-14; UNIN, 1986, p. 805; *Daily Dispatch*, 18.10.86; *Windhoek Observer*, 25.10.86
32 UNIN, 1986, p. 806; *Windhoek Observer*, 5.7.86, 25.10.86; *Star*, 3.9.86

CHAPTER 3: Economic Exploitation

1 UNIN, 1986, pp. 77, 856-7; Smith, 1986, p. 20
2 UNIN, 1987, p. 856; IDAF, 1987, p. 12
3 SWAPO Women's Solidarity Campaign, 1984, pp. 7-84
4 IDAF, 1987, pp. 7-8; Simon & Moorsom, 1986, pp. 8-9
5 Simon & Moorsom, 1987, p. 88
6 IDAF, 1987, pp. 8-9
7 Simon & Moorsom, 1987, p. 89
8 Green, 1987, pp. 5-7
9 Green, 1987, p. 65
10 CIIR, 1984, p. 4
11 *Focus*, No. 65, July-August 1986, p. 4
12 IDAF, 1987, p. 8; Department of Governmental Affairs, 1987, pp. 20-21
13 IDAF, 1987, p 18; *Focus*, No. 71, July-August 1987, p. 11
14 *Action on Namibia*, spring 1988, p. 19
15 IDAF, 1987, p. 9; *Southern Africa Focus*, February 1987
16 *Windhoek Advertiser*, 6.7.87
17 *Southern Africa Focus*, February 1987; Simon and Moorsom, 1987, p. 98
18 IDAF, 1987, pp. 18, 27-8
19 IDAF, 1987, pp. 18, 24, 28
20 IDAF, 1987, p. 9; Bureau for Research, 1987, p. 12

21 Simon & Moorsom, 1986, appendix
22 Simon & Moorsom, 1986, p. 11; Werner, 1987, p. 76
23 Van der Merwe, 1983
24 Moorsom, 1982, p 60; *Africa Insight*, Vol. 12, No. 3, 1982
25 UNIN, 1986, p. 856; Angula, 1984, p. 2
26 Angula, 1984, p. 3
27 IDAF, 1987, pp. 14-15
28 Simon, 1986
29 IDAF, 1987, p. 15; Simon & Moorsom, 1986, p. 10
30 *Windhoek Observer*, 26.1.85
31 Von Garnier, 1986, pp. 6-7
32 Merrington, 1986, pp. 4, 20
33 Merrington, 1986, pp. 50-51
34 Von Garnier, 1986, p 7; *SASPU National*, December 1987
35 *Windhoek Observer*, 17.1.87
36 Werner, 1987, p. 73
37 *Focus*, No. 68, January-February 1987, p. 11
38 IDAF, 1987, pp. 24-5
39 IDAF, 1987, pp. 24-8
40 *Focus*, No. 71, July-August 1987, p. 11
41 IDAF, 1987, p. 29
42 *Focus*, No. 63 March-April 1986, p. 10
43 Cronje & Cronje, 1979, pp. 71-2, 75-6
44 *Focus*, No.75, March-April 1988
45 IDAF, 1987, pp. 36-7
46 IDAF, 1987, p. 38
47 IDAF, 1987 p. 39
48 IDAF, 1987, p. 41
49 *Focus*, No. 68, January-February 1987, p. 11, No. 71, July-August 1987, p. 11, No. 75, March-April 1988, p. 10 *Action on Namibia*, autumn 1987
50 *Southscan*, 15.6.88; *Financial Times*, 21.6.88

CHAPTER 4: Living Conditions

1 *Windhoek Advertiser*, 21.8.87
2 IDAF, 1987, p. 31
3 UNCN, 1983, p. 6; Cawthra, 1986, p. 181, 188; UNIN, 1986, p. 418
4 IDAF, 1987, p. 31
5 *Windhoek Advertiser*, 22.10.86, 10.4.87; *Windhoek Observer*, 4.4.87
6 Von Garnier, 1987; IDAF, 1987, p. 30
7 Bureau for Research, 1987, p. 19
8 IDAF, 1985, p. 16; Simon, 1988, pp. 245-60
9 IDAF, 1987, pp. 31-3
10 UNIN, 1984, p. 20; IDAF, 1985, p. 3; Smith, 1986 p. 53
11 Smith, 1986, pp. 20, 33
12 Du Plessis, 1986, pp. 24, 26
13 *Namibian*, 12.9.86
14 IDAF, 1985, pp. 7-9; Lindsay, 1987, p. 4
15 Smith, 1986, pp. 55-6
16 *Namibia Digest*, October 1983, p. 9
17 *Focus*, No. 64 May-June 1986, p. 11
18 IDAF, 1985, p. 20; UNIN, 1986, p. 558; Andersson & Marks, 1987, p. 275; WUS, 1987, p. 8
19 IDAF, 1985, pp. 24-5

20 IDAF, 1985, p. 25; *Windhoek Advertiser*, 26.5.87
21 IDAF, 1985, p. 29
22 IDAF, 1985, p. 29
23 IDAF, 1985, pp. 29-30
24 *Focus*, May-June 1986, p. 11
25 Lobstein & NSC, 1984; IDAF, 1985, pp. 32-5
26 IDAF, 1985, p 27; IDAF, 1987, p. 25
27 *Namibian*, 22.8.86
28 Andersson & Marks, p. 290; IDAF, 1987, pp. 24-5
29 Lindsay, 1987, pp. 2-3

CHAPTER 5: Education, Information and Ideas

1 Cited in Ellis, 1984, p. 23
2 Ellis, 1984, p. 25; Abrahams, 1986, p. 26; UNIN, 1986, p. 509
3 Ellis, 1984, p. 41; Abrahams, 1986, p. 28; *Focus*, No.69, March-April 1987, p. 10
4 *Namibian*, 12.9.86
5 *Windhoek Advertiser*, 16.1.86; *Focus*, No. 71, July-August 1987, p. 10
6 Ellis, 1984, p. 84; *Windhoek Advertiser*, 17.1.85, 9.3.87; *Windhoek Observer*, 14.3.87
7 *Star*, 8.10.85; *Windhoek Advertiser*, 17.1.85
8 *Focus*, No. 63, March-April 1986, p. 11
9 CIIR, 1986, p. 34; *Windhoek Advertiser*, 17.1.87, 9.3.87; *Namibian*, 12.9.86
10 Smith, 1986 pp. 48-9
11 *Windhoek Advertiser*, 5.3.87
12 Ellis, 1984, p. 40; *Namibian*, 23.1.87
13 *CCN Information*, March-April 1987
14 *Focus*, No. 71, July-August 1987, p. 10; No. 77, July-August 1988, p. 10
15 *Focus*, No. 63, March-April 1987, p. 11; *Action on Namibia*, autumn 1987, pp. 6-7
16 *Focus*, No. 77, July-August 1958, p. 10; *Southscan*, 15.6.88; *Namibian*, 17.6.88
17 WUS, 1987, pp. 10-11
18 Ellis, 1984, p. 49; *Namibian*, 19.9.87
19 Ellis, 1984, pp. 49-50
20 Van der Merwe, 1984; *Namibian*, 19.9.87
21 *Financial Mail*, 30.8.85
22 *Combatant*, August 1986; *Namibian*, 7.11.86
23 *Namibian*, 8.11.85
24 *Focus*, No. 55, November-December 1984, p. 9
25 *Windhoek Advertiser*, 26.9.86; *Windhoek Observer*, 13.12.86
26 *Focus*, No. 75, March-April 1988, p. 11
27 IDAF, 1980, p. 41
28 CIIR, 1986, pp. 58-9
29 *CCN Information*, May 1986
30 *Focus*, No.71, July-August 1987, p. 10
31 *Windhoek Observer*, 8.2.86
32 *Namibian*, 4.7.86, 5.9.86, 7.11.86
33 SWAPO, [undated]
34 *Namibian*, 5/19.12.87, *Windhoek Advertiser*, 19.12.87
35 *Windhoek Advertiser*, 12.8.87

CHAPTER 6: Repression

1 British Council of Churches, 1981 p. 12
2 IDAF, 1980, pp. 36-7; Hortors, 1987, p. 220; Government Gazette 18.2.87
3 UN Security Council Resolution 276 of 30 January 1970
4 *Focus*, No. 60, September-October 1985, p. 10
5 *Focus*, No. 68, January-February 1987, p. 10
6 IDAF, 1980, p. 35; Amnesty International, 1982, p. 8
7 Amnesty International, 1982, p. 9
8 IDAF, 1980, p. 37
9 *Focus*, No. 62, January-February 1986, pp. 1-2, No. 61, November-December 1985, p. 10, No. 65, July-August 1986, p. 3
10 *Focus*, No. 58, May-June 1985, p. 3
11 *Focus*, No. 66, September-October 1986, p. 10
12 Amnesty International, 1982, pp. 4-5; *Focus*, No. 69, March-April 1987, p. 10
13 Amnesty International, 1982, pp. 3-4; *Focus*, No. 58, May-June 1985, p. 1
14 Amnesty International, 1982, p. 4
15 *Windhoek Advertiser*, 6.10.86; *Focus*, No. 68, Jan-Feb 1987, p. 10
16 SACBC, 1982, p. 21
17 SWAPO, 1978a, pp. 3-5; IDAF 1980, pp. 33-4
18 *Namibian*, 20.11.87
19 *Focus*, No. 58, May-June 1985, pp. 1-4, No. 68, January-February 1987, p. 10
20 SACBC, 1982, p. 21
21 British Council of Churches, 1981
22 SWAPO, 1978a pp. 5-9; Amnesty International, 1982, pp. 6-8; Cawthra, 1986, p. 214
23 *Focus*, No. 50, January-February 1984, p. 11; No. 51, March-April 1984, p. 4
24 *Focus*, No. 66, September-October 1987, p. 11, *Windhoek Observer*, 4.1.86
25 *Focus*, No. 55, September-October 1986, p. 11; *Soldier of Fortune*, April 1987, pp. 84-5
26 *Star*, 18.8.81
27 Asmal, 1980; IDAF, 1982, p. 1

CHAPTER 7: Military Occupation

1 Cawthra, 1986, p. 178
2 *Focus*, No. 73 November-December 1986, p. 4
3 *Focus*, No. 61 November-December 1985, p. 11
4 Cawthra, 1986, p. 179
5 *Cape Times*, 4.1.85
6 Cawthra, 1986, pp. 176-98
7 Cawthra, 1986 pp. 131-2
8 *Focus*, No. 61 November-December 1985, p. 11
9 Cawthra, 1986, pp. 199-204
10 Soggot, 1986 pp. 96-116

11 Konig, 1983, pp. 42-9; Cawthra, 1986, pp. 210-12; Soggot, 1986
12 Konig, 1986, pp. 44-5, 53; *Focus*, No. 70, May-June 1987, p. 4
13 *Focus*, No. 70, May-June 1987, p. 4
14 *Focus*, No. 76, May-June 1988, p. 11
15 Konig, 1983, pp. 42-9; Cawthra, 1986, pp. 210-14; *Focus*, No. 66, September-October 1986, p. 11; No. 70, May-June 1987, p. 11
16 Cawthra, 1986, pp. 26-31, 204-5
17 *Focus*, No. 73, November-December 1987, p. 4
18 *Focus*, No. 63, March-April 1986, p. 11
19 *Focus*, No. 71, July-August 1987, p. 10
20 Cawthra, 1986 pp. 131, 148, 205-6; *Focus*, No. 63, March-April 1987, p. 10
21 *Focus*, No. 73, November-December 1987, p. 4
22 Hanlon, 1986, p. 1
23 Hanlon, 1986, pp. 156-9; Wolfers & Bergerol, 1983
24 Hanlon, 1986, pp. 158-9; Holness, 1986, pp. 94-5
25 Holness, 1986, pp. 98-100; Cawthra, 1986, pp. 150-51
26 Holness, 1986, pp. 101-2; Cawthra, 1986 p. 154
27 Holness, 1986 pp. 102-4; Cawthra, 1986 p. 159
28 *Focus*, No. 63, March-April 1986, p. 12; No. 67, November-December 1986, p. 12; No. 71, July-August 1987, p. 12; No. 72, September-October 1987, p. 12; No. 74, January-February 1988, p. 12
29 Hanlon, 1986 pp. 244-5; Cawthra, 1986 pp. 173-4
30 *Focus*, No. 68, November-December 1987, p. 12
31 Hanlon, 1986, p. 245
32 *Focus*, No. 65, July-August 1986, No. 71, July-August 1987
33 Hanlon, 1986, pp. 222-3
34 Cawthra, 1986, pp. 172, 175; *Focus*, No. 65, July-August 1986, p. 5; No. 71, July-August 1971, p. 12

CHAPTER 8: Liberation Struggle

1 SWAPO, 1981, pp. 165-6; Katjavivi, 1984, pp. 9-13; Werner, 1984, pp. 5-10; Katjavivi, 1988, pp. 24-5
2 SWAPO, 1981, p. 167
3 SWAPO, 1981, pp. 168-9
4 Katjavivi, 1984, pp. 17-18
5 Katjavivi, 1984, pp. 19-20
6 Katjavivi, 1984, p. 20
7 SWAPO, 1981, pp. 172-4; Katjavivi, 1984, pp. 21-30
8 SWAPO, 1978b, pp. 13-14; Soggot, 1986, pp. 24-32
9 SWAPO, 1978b, pp. 13-18; SWAPO, 1981, p. 179
10 Murray-Hudson, 1983, p. 120
11 SWAPO, 1978b, pp. 21-8; Katjavivi, 1984, pp. 35-55; Soggot, 1986, pp. 76-85
12 SWAPO, 1976
13 SWAPO, 1976, p. 6; SWAPO, 1978b, p. 28; O'Linn, 1986, p. 42
14 SWAPO, 1978, pp. 31-2

15 Cawthra, 1986, pp. 18-19
16 SWAPO, 1981, p. 178; Katjavivi, 1988, p. 84
17 SWAPO, 1981, pp. 201-5; Cawthra, 1986, pp. 179-80
18 SWAPO, 1981, pp. 221-2; Cawthra, 1986, pp. 191-2
19 *Windhoek Observer*, 5.12.87
20 Cawthra, 1986, p. 191
21 *IDAF Briefing Paper*, No.14, November 1984, No.15, March 1985, No.20, May 1986, No. 22, March 1987
22 Cawthra, 1986, p. 176
23 *IDAF Briefing Paper*, No.22, March 1987, No.23, May 1988
24 Soggot, 1986, pp. 53-107
25 SWAPO, 1981, pp. 212-31; Soggot pp. 112-204
26 SWAPO, 1981 pp. 232-3
27 Du Pisani, 1986 pp. 356-77
28 SWAPO, 1981 pp. 239-40; Soggot pp. 208-26
29 *IDAF Briefing Paper*, No.20, May 1986; No.22, March 1987; No.23, May 1988
30 SWAPO, 1980, p. 6
31 SWAPO, 1981, p. 215; Landis, 1984
32 UN, 1983, p. 19; Landis, 1984, p. 7; Katjavivi, 1988, p. 100
33 Du Pisani, 1986, p. 336
34 UN, 1983 pp. 24-6; UNIN, 1987, p. 213
35 Moorsom, 1984, p. 14
36 Landis, 1984, p. 9
37 SWAPO, 1980, p. 6
38 UNCN, 1983, p. 5
39 SWAPO, 1981, p. 244; UN, 1983, pp. 26-7; UNIN, 1987, pp. 214-16
40 UNCN, 1983, p. 6
41 UN, 1983, pp. 29-31; UNIN, 1987, p. 219
42 UNCN, 1983, p. 8; Minty, 1986, p. 4
43 UNCN, 1983, p. 8; UNIN, 1987, p. 220
44 Cawthra, 1986, pp. 150-51; Minty, 1986, pp. 5-6
45 UNCN, 1983, pp. 17-19; Minty, 1986, pp. 7-8; Cawthra, 1986, p. 184
46 UNCN, 1983, p. 19; Landis, 1984, pp. 10-11; Minty, 1986, p. 8; Cawthra, 1986, p. 184
47 UNIN, 1987, pp. 223-4
48 Minty, 1986, p. 9
49 Cawthra, 1986, pp. 154-5
50 Cawthra, 1986 pp. 184-5
51 *IDAF Briefing Paper*, No.12, July 1984
52 *IDAF Briefing Paper*, No.12, July 1984; UNIN, 1987, pp. 226-7
53 *IDAF Briefing Paper*, No.20, May 1986 p. 6; Minty, 1986 p. 13
54 Minty, 1986, pp. 13-14
55 *Focus*, No. 77, July-August 1988, p. 9
56 *Namibian*, 6.11.87
57 *Focus*, No. 77, July-August 1988, p. 11
58 Simon and Moorsom, 1987
59 Cawthra, 1986, pp. 181-93
60 *Focus*, No. 73, November-December 1987, p. 4
61 *Action on Namibia*, winter 1986-7, p. 5
62 *Focus* No. 63, March-April 1986, p. 11; No. 67, November-December 1986, p. 10; No. 77, July-August 1988, p. 10
63 *Focus*, No. 71, July-August 1987, p. 11; No. 72, September-October 1987, p. 9; No. 73, November-December 1987, p. 3; *Namibian*, 17.6.88
64 Strauss, 1987

INDEX

Individual laws are indexed collectively under legislation

WORKING UNDER SOUTH AFRICAN OCCUPATION

Labour in Namibia

Fact Paper No. 14

IDAF Research, Information and Publications Department

'Much still has to be done to explain how employers in Namibia regard their workers as non-human units of labour power . . . the facts in this booklet should go a long way to enlighten people.' AEU JOURNAL.

Outlines the basic facts about the Namibian economy and workforce, examines the migrant labour system, discrimination and living conditions, and describes the struggle to organise trade unions in the face of police and army repression.

1987   £1.00 $8^{1}/_{4}$ x $5^{3}/_{4}$"   49pp.

ISBN 0 904759 73 3   Book No. D098

INTERNATIONAL DEFENCE AND AID FUND FOR SOUTHERN AFRICA
Canon Collins House, 64 Essex Road, London N1 8LR

"The specific mandate of IDAF is to ensure the legal defence of the victims of apartheid, to aid their families and dependents, and to inform the world about apartheid and the struggle against it.

There can be no real peace in Southern Africa until the peoples of Namibia and South Africa have been liberated. South Africa attacks neighbouring states causing widespread destruction and suffering. Opponents of apartheid living abroad have become targets for assassinations and massacres.

In South Africa and Namibia, the heightened repression has placed increasing demands on the work of IDAF. Behind a curtain of censorship and legislation, the trials and imprisonment, the detention and torture, the forced removals and bannings, the violence and killings go on remorselessly, at a more terrible level than ever before.

A very special concern of IDAF is the children, who have been made the particular target of the apartheid regime, and face a calculated and brutal onslaught from its armed forces and police.

We urgently need your support. Make your contribution to a free, just and peaceful Southern Africa. Send your donation, large or small, to our Fund at its Head Office at the address above, or to one of the addresses."

Archbishop Trevor Huddleston, Chair of the Trustees of IDAF

The International Defence and Aid Fund for Southern Africa is a humanitarian organisation founded by Canon L John Collins, dedicated to the achievement of free, democratic, non-racial societies in South Africa and Namibia.

The International Defence and Aid Fund for Southern Africa is associated with a registered English charity, The Sol Plaatje Educational Project Limited, which assists with the education of children who are victims of apartheid.

IDAF has National Committees in various countries. Their accounts are audited and they are part of the Fund. For convenience supporters may wish to send contributions to them at the following addresses: please address your donation to Archbishop Trevor Huddleston.

CANADA
IDAFSA-Canada
294 Albert St #200
Ottowa, K1P 6E6
Tel: (613)-233-5939

IRELAND
IDAFSA-Ireland
PO Box 1974
Dublin 18
Tel: (01) 895035

NETHERLANDS
DAF-Nederland
Kromme Nieuwegracht 10
3512 HG Utrecht
Tel: (30) 313194
Postgiro a/c no: 2989732-Hilversum

NEW ZEALAND
NZDAF
PO Box 17303
Karori
Wellington 5

NORWAY
IDAF-Norway
PO Box 2
Lindeberg Gaard
N-1007 Oslo 10
Tel: (2) 301345
Postgiro a/c no: 2616670

SWEDEN
Swedish Defence and Aid Fund
c/o Lennart Renöfelt,
Månskensgatan 34F,
80274 GAULE
Postgiro a/c no: 4093290-7

UNITED KINGDOM
BDAFSA
22 The Ivories
6-8 Northampton Street
London N1 2HX
Tel: (01) 354 1462
Postgiro a/c no: 5 11 7151

UNITED STATES OF AMERICA
IDAFSA-US
PO Box 17
Cambridge, Ma 02138
Tel: (617) 491 8343